ESTHER

Ideas A to Z Series

26 Fun-filled Learning Activities on Bible Characters

ESTHER

Phyllis Vos Wezeman, Anna L. Liechty, and Judith Harris Chase

Grand Rapids, MI 49501

Ideas A–Z Series: Esther by Phyllis Vos Wezeman, Anna L. Liechty, and Judith Harris Chase

© 1997 by Kregel Publications

Published by Kregel Publications, a division of Kregel Inc., P.O. Box 2607, Grand Rapids, MI 49501. Kregel Publications provides trusted, biblical publications for Christian growth and service. Your comments and suggestions are valued.

All rights reserved. No part of this book may be reproduced, stored in a retrieval system, or transmitted in any form or by any means—electronic, mechanical, photocopy, recording, or otherwise—without written permission of the publisher, except for brief quotations in printed reviews.

Unless otherwise indicated, Scripture quotations are from the *Holy Bible: New International Version*®. Copyright © 1973, 1978, 1984 by International Bible Society. Used by permission of Zondervan Publishing House. All rights reserved.

Cover illustration: Patrick Kelley, © 1997
Cover design: Alan G. Hartman
Book design: Nicholas G. Richardson

Library of Congress Cataloging-in-Publication Data
Wezeman, Phyllis Vos.
  The Ideas A–Z Series: Esther / Phyllis Vos Wezeman, Anna L. Liechty, Judith Harris Chase.
    p.   cm.   (Ideas A to Z series; 1)
  Includes bibliographical references.
  1. Bible. O.T. Esther—Study and teaching. 2. Christian education of children. I. Liechty, Anna L. II. Title. III. Series
BS1375.5.W48   1997   222'.909505—dc21   96-6581
                                                                            CIP
ISBN 0-8254-3961-2

Printed in the United States of America
1 2 3 / 03 02 01 00 99 98 97

To my great aunts and uncles, the sisters and brothers
of my grandma, Esther Tromp, who helped teach me
the importance of family (P.V.W.)
Mae La Bow
Minnie Szarat
Wilbert Chaloupka
LeRoy (Ted) Chaloupka
Alice Fencl

To my sister Nancy Bach Fowler,
who, like Esther, knows what it means to stand alone with God (A.L.L.)

To the girls I had as students
at the South Hebrew Day School,
who demonstrate Esther's true beauty by courageously and
faithfully following spiritual teachings (J.H.C.)

CONTENTS

	Introduction	8
	Overview	9
A:	Attributes	14
B:	Books	15
C:	Costumes	17
D:	Death	21
E:	Environment	23
F:	Foods	24
G:	Geography	27
H:	Hangman	28
I:	Intercession	30
J:	Jewish Holidays	32
K:	Key Verse	42
L:	Lots	44
M:	Megillah	46
N:	Notes	48
O:	Obedience	50
P:	Puppets	51
Q:	Questions	59
R:	Rhythm Story	60
S:	Storytelling	62
T:	Trips	64
U:	Uniqueness	66
V:	Verse	67
W:	Writing	69
X:	Xerxes	70
Y:	Year	72
Z:	Zeresh Plus	74
	Resources	76

INTRODUCTION

Taking a look at the shelves in Christian bookstores, one can almost come to a conclusion that writers of religious education books have taken too literally God's command to be fruitful and multiply! With the deluge of available materials, why on earth do we offer the *Ideas A–Z* series?

First of all, *Ideas A–Z* provides an in-depth look at Scripture, at both the people and the important themes. Using twenty-six different view points assures readers of thoughtful and thorough reflections on Bible topics. Each perspective provides opportunities for experiencing the lesson on a variety of levels, allowing readers and participants to discover the story in a way appropriate to their stages in life and faith development.

Ideas A–Z also develops a unique format for delivering insights, information, and activities. The A–Z topics offer a balanced variety of methods and approaches for experiencing the Bible story. For every letter of the alphabet there is a different theme and a different way of exploring that theme, like puppetry, music, drama, games, or storytelling. Such experiential learning also takes into consideration the needs of all learning styles.

Another aspect of the format is its flexibility. Each idea, A–Z, can be used alone or combined with ideas from other letters to develop a lesson plan, a worship experience, or an intergenerational activity. The ideas can simply be used to supplement existing curricula, or they can be referred to like a handbook. The format is user-friendly and open-ended, providing essential information yet fostering creative applications.

From beginning students of the Bible to more advanced learners, *Ideas A–Z* can inspire and motivate participants to keep looking at the Scriptures in fresh ways and keep applying the Bible's principles to their own lives.

So although Esther's story has been told and retold, *Ideas A–Z* offers today's descendants of Esther an opportunity to explore and experience the adventure from beginning to end, from A to Z. Like Esther, our experience will lead us to be faithful to the God who loves us and preserves us in the trials of life.

OVERVIEW

WHO?

Who is Esther? Esther is an exile, orphan, cousin, niece, candidate, queen, wife, subject, Jew, intercessor, advocate, savior, ruler—and example.

Esther, daughter of Abihail, was a descendent of the exiles taken to Babylon in 597 B.C. As an orphan, she was raised by her relative Mordecai. Some commentators suggest that Esther was Mordecai's niece, while others say that she was his cousin. Regardless of the relationship, Mordecai treated Esther as his own daughter, and he loved her very much.

Esther started out as a candidate in the beauty contest to find a replacement for King Xerxes' deposed queen, Vashti, and was chosen to become the ruler's new wife and queen. Although she was the queen, she was also the king's subject, a fact that became evident during the threat to annihilate the entire Jewish population in Persia.

After Mordecai explained Haman's wicked plot to Esther, she interceded with the king to spare the lives of the people of Israel. She then revealed that she too was a Jew. Not only was Esther an advocate, she was also the savior of God's people. In the end, she became a ruler as she executed orders to spare the Jews and to celebrate the victory.

Most importantly, Esther is an example. Esther was a woman used by God to accomplish His purposes. She was a woman who allowed God to use her "for such a time as this." Esther is a reminder that, with God's guidance, one person can make a difference in the world.

WHAT?

Summary of the Story

Nearly five hundred years before Jesus was born, the Israelite people were exiled to the land of Persia. Although in Esther's time they were free to return to their homeland, many Jews remained in Persia because they had jobs and family there. As the book of Esther begins, King Xerxes, the powerful ruler of Persia, is holding a banquet for his officials. One day, the king ordered Queen Vashti to appear at the banquet so the guests could see her great beauty. Queen Vashti refused to come, and because of her disobedience she was banished from the palace.

Some time later, the king was sad and lonely. His advisors suggested that he hold a contest to find the most beautiful woman in the whole land to become the next queen. Mordecai, a Jewish man who held a position just outside the palace, had a beautiful relative named Esther, who was taken to the palace to be seen by the king. When the king met Esther, he chose her to be the new queen.

Although Esther then lived in the palace, she saw Mordecai frequently. One day Mordecai overheard some servants plotting to kill the king, and he told Esther of the plan. After Esther gave the information to the king, the story was recorded in the royal records of the country.

Another man in the palace, Haman, the prime minister, was a very powerful person in Persia. Unfortunately, Haman was a wicked, evil man. One day, he demanded that everyone must bow down to him whenever they saw him. Mordecai, a devout Jew who only worshipped God, refused. In his anger, Haman told King Xerxes that the Jews were planning to murder the king. Haman tricked the king into agreeing to kill all of the Jews in Persia. Then Haman cast lots to determine the day of the slaughter and prepared for the execution, including building a gallows on which to hang Mordecai.

When Mordecai heard the horrible news of the plan to massacre his people, he put on sackcloth and ashes and began to mourn. Mordecai told Esther that she must go to the king to plead for mercy for the Jewish people. Esther asked the Jewish people to fast and pray for three days as she prepared to visit the king. It was a law in Persia that no one—not even the queen—could approach the king without an invitation, and the penalty for breaking this rule was death. Esther, trusting in God, went to the royal chamber where the king sat on his throne. When King Xerxes noticed Esther, he held out his royal scepter, which meant that it was safe for her to advance. When the king asked Esther what she wanted, she invited him to a banquet and asked him to bring Haman too. At the banquet, Esther did not reveal her request. Instead she invited the two men to another meal.

That night, the king could not sleep, and he asked for the royal records to be read to him. He was reminded of Mordecai's good deed.

At the second feast, Esther asked the king for mercy for her people and for herself. She told the king that she was a Jew too. When the king asked who devised such a wicked plot, Esther pointed the finger at Haman.

Not only did the king grant Esther's request to spare the lives of the Jewish people, King Xerxes ordered Haman to be hung on the gallows that he had built to hang Mordecai. Mordecai was given the place of honor in the palace that Haman had held. The Jewish people celebrated their deliverance and God's faithfulness to them with an observance called Purim, the Feast of Lots, that is still commemorated every year.

WHEN?

Timeline

A timeline provides a way to put the events of history in order—to actually visualize what happened at what point in time. Because the Christian world uses the birth of Jesus to divide and date history, abbreviations in a timeline often include B.C. and A.D.; B.C. stands for "before Christ," and A.D., the Latin words *anno Domini*, means "in the year of our Lord." The letters *ca.*, an abbreviation for *circa*, before a date means around or about that year. It is important to note that dates vary depending on the reference material used to compile a timeline. Use the timeline provided as a guide for putting Bible events into perspective, but refer to additional resources to supplement the information.

Undated	Creation
Undated	Adam and Eve; the Fall; Cain and Abel
Undated	Noah; the Flood
Undated	Tower of Babel
2100 B.C.	Abraham
2066 B.C.	Abraham and Isaac
2006 B.C.	Jacob and Esau
1900 B.C.	Joseph in Egypt
1700–1250 B.C.	Hebrews in Egypt
1526 B.C.	Moses born
1450 B.C.	the Exodus; Moses and the Law
1399 B.C.	Joshua; the Promised Land
1375 B.C.	judges begin to rule Israel
1209 B.C.	Deborah
1162 B.C.	Gideon
1105 B.C.	Samuel born
1070 B.C.	Samson
1050 B.C.	Saul becomes Israel's first king
1000–961 B.C.	David reigns as king
970 B.C.	Solomon becomes king

959 B.C.	the temple in Jerusalem completed
930 B.C.	the kingdom of Israel divides
875 B.C.	Elijah and the prophets
793 B.C.	Jonah
740 B.C.	Isaiah
605 B.C.	Daniel
586 B.C.	Jerusalem and the temple destroyed
537 B.C.	first Jewish exiles return from captivity
516 B.C.	new temple completed in Jerusalem
479 B.C.	Mordecai, Esther, and Haman
445 B.C.	Nehemiah builds Jerusalem wall
333 B.C.	Judea made part of Greek empire
63 B.C.	Rome occupies Judea
40–4 B.C.	Herod the Great, king of Judea
7–4 B.C.	Jesus born
A.D. 26/27	John the Baptist preaches
A.D. 26/27	Jesus baptized
A.D. 30	the Crucifixion
A.D. 30	Pentecost
A.D. 35	Paul converted
A.D. 40	James martyred
A.D. 45	Paul's journeys begin
A.D. 45–90	letters to Christians
A.D. 67	Paul martyred
A.D. 70	Romans destroy Jerusalem
A.D. 96	all books of New Testament completed

ESTHER: Ideas A–Z Series

WHERE?

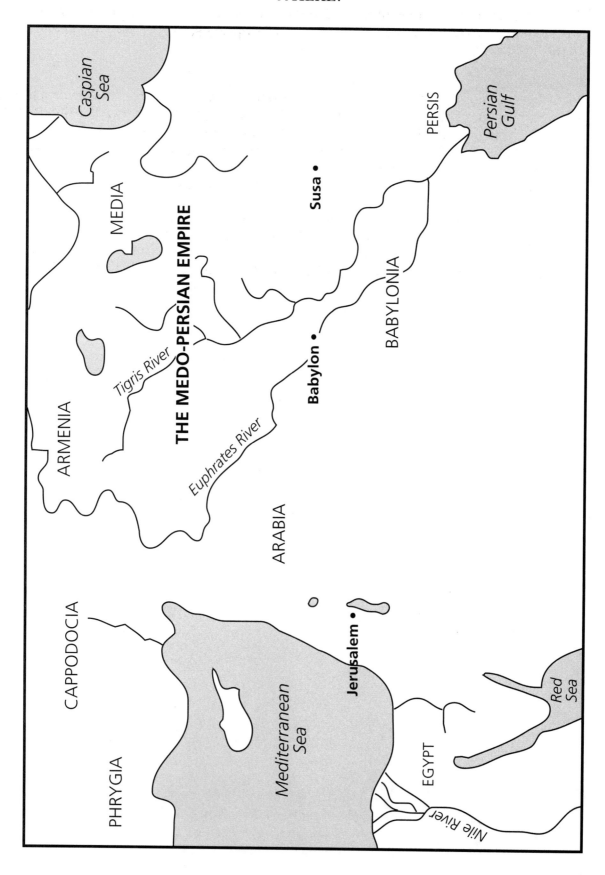

Scripture Passages

Ten chapters in the seventeenth book of the Old Testament chronicle the events of the life of Esther. There are no additional references to Esther anywhere else in Scripture. Review the passages before leading a lesson on the life of Esther.

WHY?

The book of Esther contains one of the most interesting, dramatic stories in the Scriptures, but it is much more than drama. It is the history of how God delivered His people from a holocaust. The Bible is full of stories of God's salvation and deliverance. God's goodness and mercy is evident everywhere. What distinguishes the Esther story is that the destiny of God's people lies in the hands of one person. One faithful, courageous young woman was instrumental in saving an entire nation.

While the book of Esther does not mention the name of God, it is obvious that this is—and was intended to be—a story of God's saving love and power. The key verse, 4:14, ". . . And who knows but that you have come to royal position for such a time as this?" implies that there is a divine plan in the position in which Esther finds herself. God chose the weak and relatively insignificant one to save His people. This is not so much a story about Esther's beauty as it is a story about the beauty of God's saving power. It is not so much about Esther's faithfulness to her people as it is about God's faithfulness to His people.

A
ATTRIBUTES

Purpose
To encourage readers to see the hidden characteristics of Esther and to use the information in an A–Z poem

Preparation
- Paper
- Pencils
- Dictionary
- Thesaurus

Procedure
With the very first reading, we can recognize that the book of Esther is a good story. But why? What attributes make the story a good drama? If we look below the surface and begin to analyze, we recognize there is a force working behind the scenes to create a message of value. There are elements of romance, intrigue, and danger to heighten our interest. There is a complex plot featuring a nasty villain, several ironic reversals, and the ultimate triumph of good over evil. We increase our appreciation of the story and its Author when we look for the hidden qualities of good drama that drive our interest.

Just as there is more to a story than words, there is more to the person of Esther than just her beauty. It is interesting that a Persian interpretation of the meaning of the name *Esther* is "star." A related Hebrew word results in interpreting her name to mean "hidden." What made her stand out among all the beautiful women of Persia? It was not only her "star" quality. She had other, hidden attributes as well.

After reading the story of Esther, guide participants to think below the surface-level meaning and search for attributes of Esther that make her inspirational. Use these attributes to create an A–Z poem.

Begin the poem with the words "Esther was." Then, for every letter of the alphabet, brainstorm adjectives that describe attributes seen in Esther's behavior, attitude, and actions that make her beautiful because of her inner qualities. Use a dictionary or thesaurus to help locate words. Consider assigning small groups several letters to brainstorm, and compile the poem as a cooperative effort. Remind participants to look beyond outward appearance. For example, for the letter *A*, they would choose an adjective like *accepting* over *attractive*. *B* might be *brave* or *bold*, *C* could be *cautious*, *courageous*, or *courteous*, *D*, *devoted*, and so forth.

Share the individual poems or cooperative projects with the entire group. Write the words on a piece of paper in the form of a scroll and display the finished product for others to review.

B

BOOKS

Purpose
To review the books of the Bible and to note that Esther is the twelfth book of history and the seventeenth book of the Old Testament

Preparation
- Bibles
- Matchboxes, large and small
- Adhesive-backed paper
- Scissors
- Rulers
- Fine-tipped permanent markers

Procedure
Although the story of Esther is contained in one book of the Bible, in order to find these ten chapters, it is helpful to know the books of the Bible in order. Review the books of the Old Testament and the New Testament—in sequence—and use the activity to create a mini-library!

Old Testament

Pentateuch
Genesis
Exodus
Leviticus
Numbers
Deuteronomy

History
Joshua
Judges
Ruth
1 Samuel
2 Samuel
1 Kings
2 Kings
1 Chronicles
2 Chronicles
Ezra
Nehemiah
Esther

Writings
Job
Psalms
Proverbs
Ecclesiastes
Song of Solomon

Major Prophets
Isaiah
Jeremiah
Lamentations
Ezekiel
Daniel

Minor Prophets
Hosea
Joel
Amos
Obadiah
Jonah
Micah
Habakkuk
Zephaniah
Haggai
Zechariah
Malachi

ESTHER: Ideas A–Z Series

New Testament

Gospels
Matthew
Mark
Luke
John

History
Acts

Pauline Epistles to Churches
Romans
1 Corinthians
2 Corinthians
Galatians
Ephesians
Philippians
Colossians
1 Thessalonians
2 Thessalonians

Pauline Epistles to Individuals
1 Timothy
2 Timothy
Titus
Philemon

General Epistles
Hebrews
James
1 Peter
2 Peter
1 John
2 John
3 John
Jude
Revelation

Select a small kitchen matchbox for each book of the Bible—sixty-six of them! Cover two sides and the "spine" of each box with adhesive-backed paper to form a book jacket. To create the pages, cut a narrow strip of white paper and glue it around the remaining portion of each box. Draw lines on the white paper to represent pages. Write the name of the book on the spine of each volume. Sequence the minibooks by standing them side by side in order.

As a handy way to keep the individual volumes together, cover several large kitchen matchboxes with adhesive-backed paper. Stand the smaller boxes inside of the larger ones and place them end-to-end.

To reduce the number of boxes necessary for the project, do the Old Testament in one session and the New Testament at another time or create a volume for each major division of the Old Testament and the New Testament instead of for each specific book.

Note that Esther is the twelfth book of history and the seventeenth book of the Old Testament. Since Esther became queen in 479 B.C., the book bearing her name was probably written around 473–471 B.C. While Esther follows Nehemiah in the Bible, its events are about thirty years prior to those recorded in Nehemiah. Although the author is unknown, the writer could have been Mordecai or another Jew living in Persia who might have made use of records kept by Mordecai. Some scholars suggest Ezra or Nehemiah as the author because of the similarity of writing style. It is interesting to note that Esther is one of only two books in the Bible named for women. Ruth is the other one. Ruth records the story of a Gentile woman who marries a Jewish man, Boaz; Esther records the account of a Jewish woman who becomes the wife of a Gentile king, Ahasuerus, also called Xerxes I. It is also unusual that in the original version no name, title, or pronoun for God appears in the book of Esther. Although God's name is not mentioned, God's presence is clear throughout the story, and the account clearly demonstrates God's sovereignty and His loving care for His people.

C

COSTUMES

Purpose
To underscore the importance of costumes in the celebration of Purim and to provide simple patterns for clothing, masks, and hats

Preparation
- Materials vary for each costume, mask, and hat

Procedure
Dominating the Purim celebration is drama. In addition to the reenactment of the story of Esther, other dramatic events might feature puppet shows, melodramas, skits, and role playing.

Costumes are a vital part of these festivities. Children dress up in all types of costumes—clowns, princesses, and superheroes are popular. Many adults, as well as children, portray one of the principal characters from the story of Esther. The Bible gives clues about the clothing worn by Esther and Mordecai. In Esther 2:17 and 5:1, we read that she had a crown and wore royal robes. It is recorded that Mordecai wore a garment of sackcloth as he mourned the fate of his people. He was given new clothing when he was honored by the king. "Mordecai left the king's presence wearing royal garments of blue and white, a large crown of gold and a purple robe of fine linen" (Esther 8:15).

Fashion garments from paper or fabric using available supplies and no-sew techniques.

PAPER-BAG COSTUMES

Preparation
- Large grocery bags
- Pencils
- Scissors
- Tape
- Yarn
- Markers
- Stapler and staples
- Paper scraps

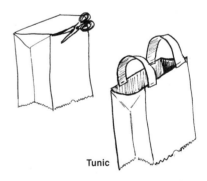
Tunic

Procedure
For a tunic, cut the bottom from the bag and cut out half circles at the sides for the arms. Make shoulder straps of paper or yarn to hold the bag on the body. To create a royal cape, cut an opening up the center front of a grocery bag and cut a circle for the neck. Use markers, ribbons, or cut paper trims to decorate the garments. Cover staples with tape to protect the children from sharp edges.

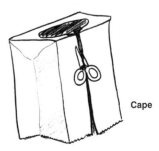
Cape

ESTHER: Ideas A–Z Series

NO-SEW TUNIC

Preparation
- Fabric or large rolls of soft paper table covering
- Pencils
- Scissors
- Tape measure
- Glue
- Iron
- Fusible web
- Wide ribbon or strips of fabric
- Miscellaneous trims
- Safety pins

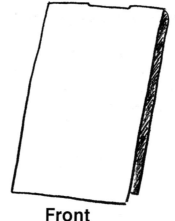
Front

Back

Procedure
Most costumes can start with a simple tunic form. Cut a rectangle of cloth (or paper) twice the height of the person from chin to floor. The piece should be almost as wide as the stretch of the person's arms. Fold the material in half and cut an 8-inch slice along the center of the folded edge for a neck opening. Cut a vertical slit down the back so the garment will fit over the head more easily. Pin the opening to fit.

Adapt the basic costume to various characters by adding a sash or by layering or draping fabric. Fabric that is cut as wide as the stretch of a person's arms will appear to have sleeves. Fabric that is cut narrower will form a sleeveless tunic. Embellish garments with trims in keeping with each role. For Esther, a long-sleeved knit top or blouse could go under a sleeveless tunic. Add trousers under a shorter tunic for Haman. Use interesting fabrics for royal-looking capes, shawls, veils, and robes.

In most cases, garments will not need sewing; however, fusible web can be used for quick construction and for attaching trims. Follow directions that come with the product. Use safety pins for fastening and altering costumes. Check costume or fashion books for accurate design details.

MASKS

Preparation
- Posterboard, half-masks, or paper plates for mask base
- Pencils
- Scissors
- Glue
- Permanent markers
- Paper scraps
- Yarn or ribbon
- Hole punch
- Trims such as feathers, sequins, faux jewels
- Paints and brushes
- Plain paper

Procedure
There are numerous kinds of disguises created and worn for Purim masquerades. Instructions for easy-to-make masks follow. It might help to draw the facial expression on a piece of paper before beginning mask construction.

HALF-MASK, READY-MADE

Purchase small masks wherever party supplies are sold. Embellish with trims that fit the character being portrayed. Use glue to attach decorations.

HALF-MASK, POSTERBOARD OR PAPER PLATE

Copy the shape of the mask illustrated on a piece of colorful posterboard large enough to fit across the wearer's eyes. Check to see that the openings for the eyes are in the correct position. Cut out the shape, punch holes on each side, and attach ribbon or yarn for ties. Decorate as needed.

Use the same method with a large paper plate cut in half. It may help the mask to fit more comfortably if a semicircle is cut out above the nose. Try on the mask and trim openings to adjust.

WHOLE-FACE MASK, PAPER PLATE

Make a simple paper plate mask that covers the whole face. Cut a slit into the rim of the plate. Overlap the two cut ends and staple or tape together to form a chin. Cut out eyes and draw or glue on a nose, lashes and eyebrows. Cut a mouth opening and paint or draw the shape of the lips. Glue on paper or yarn curls along the top of the plate—and along the bottom, if the person being portrayed has a beard. Punch holes on both sides of the mask to attach yarn or ribbon ties.

HATS AND HEADDRESSES

Preparation
- Assorted papers
- Gold-foil posterboard
- Assorted fabrics
- Pencils
- Scissors
- Rulers
- Glue
- Tape
- Stapler and staples
- Safety pins
- Faux jewels, gold chain, and gold coins
- Old felt hats
- Plan paper
- Assorted trims

ESTHER: Ideas A–Z Series

Procedure

Hats and headdresses can give identity to any number of characters in a dramatic setting. The four main people in the Purim story—Queen Esther, King Xerxes, Mordecai, and Haman—have different head coverings. Refer to books with illustrations of clothing worn in ancient Persia. Make these simple hats or create some different styles.

QUEEN ESTHER

Crowns can be as elaborate or as simple as time and resources allow. The traditional crown is a familiar style, but the Persian headpieces were probably different. Costume resources show the crown as taller and more of a cylinder shape. Some crowns fit around the head and flare out at the top. Any one of these styles can be constructed from foil-covered posterboard. Crown strips will have to be at least 22 inches long to fit around a person's head. Form a circle and staple or tape where the ends overlap. To give a more delicate look to the crown, scallop the top edge and decorate with jewels.

To complete Esther's headdress, add sheer fabric to extend from the crown. Add fringe or gold braid around the edges to give a look of elegance. Gold coins were worn on chains or bands that rested on the forehead and that were suspended under the chin.

KING XERXES

Follow the same directions to make a posterboard crown for the king. Make the cylinder a little taller and wider at the top. Cut rectangular or pointed shapes along the top edge to give a more masculine style to the crown. Another type of headpiece can be fashioned from the crown portion of an old felt hat. Fold a strip of luxurious fabric into a band about 4 inches by 22 inches; then glue or pin it to the felt hat. Tuck in the ends where the ends of the strip overlap.

MORDECAI

Many costume books show that a very common head covering for men during Esther's time was some form of turban. Choose fabric that matches or contrasts Mordecai's costume. One way to make a turban is to roll fabric—about 30 inches in length—into a tube, then begin twisting it slightly. Fit the twisted cloth around the person's head and tuck the ends inside. Pin the ends in place so the turban will hold its shape. This roll could be glued to a felt hat form, as well.

HAMAN

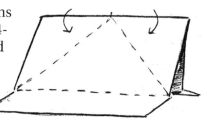

Traditionally, Haman wore a three-cornered hat. Follow the instructions to make a hat from wrapping paper, crepe paper, or stiff fabric. Fold a 14-by-22-inch sheet of the paper in half. Find the midpoint along the folded edge, pick up a top corner and fold it down. Do the same with the second corner. Raise the rim on both sides and fold to form a band. Fold the band up one more time to hold the hat together.

Finish by folding the corners to the inside, then glue in place.

Fold down corners and glue

ESTHER: Ideas A–Z Series

DEATH

Purpose
To use books to address the theme of death found throughout the story of Esther

Preparation
- Books dealing with death

Procedure
It is almost impossible to read the book of Esther or to teach a session on the story without addressing the theme of death. Mordecai learns of a plot to kill King Xerxes; Esther risks her life to save the Jewish people; Haman is hung on the gallows he built for Mordecai. These examples are just a few of the references to death found in this historical book of the Bible.

Rather than ignore the topic of death and dying, learn ways to address it. Introducing children and youth to issues of death can be aided by the use of a very accessible and attainable tool: books. The subject matter contained in this medium scans numerous themes related to end-of-life issues.

Books may be read to children by adults, offered as electives, or assigned as reports. They may be obtained from libraries, resource centers, book stores, and publishers. A selection of books set up in a special place in the classroom or home should encourage children to explore them at their own pace. It is, of course, recommended that teachers and parents read the books before they are made available to the children. This enables adults to be prepared to answer questions that might arise and to deal with feelings that may surface.

Many books are suggested as resources on issues of death. This is only a starting point, as numerous other titles and topics are available.

BOOKS ON DEATH AND DYING

Living Through the Loss of Someone You Love, Sandra P. Aldrich (Gospel Light, 1990)

The Last Thing We Talk About, Joseph Bayly (Cook Communications Ministries, 1969)

Jonathan, You Left Too Soon, David Biebel (Revel, 1996)

Andrew, You Died Too Soon: A Family Experience of Grieving and Living Again, Corinne Chilstrom (Augsburg/Fortress, 1994)

When Someone You Love Dies, William L. Coleman (Augsburg/Fortress, 1994)

Song for Sarah, P. Darcy (Harold Shaw, 1995)

Let Me Grieve but Not Forever, Verdell Davis (Word, 1989)

Mommy Please Don't Cry, L. Deymaz (Multnomah, 1996)

Helping Children Cope With Death, Robert V. Dodd (Herald Press, 1984)

Facing the Death of a Loved One, Elizabeth Elliot (Crossway Books, 1982)

When You Lose Someone You Love, Richard Exley (Honor Books, 1991)

Facing Death and the Life After, Billy Graham (Word, 1989)

I'll Hold You in Heaven, Jack Hayford (Gospel Light, 1986)

Helping Children Grieve: When Someone They Love Dies, T. Huntley (Augsburg/Fortress, 1991)

When Will I Stop Hurting? June Cerza Kolf (Baker, 1987)

Life After Grief, Lawrenz and Gree (Baker, 1995)

A Grief Observed, C. S. Lewis (Bantam Books, 1983)

Coming to Grips With Death and Dying, Erwin Lutzer (Moody Press, 1992)

Winter Grief, Summer Grace, James Miller (Augsburg Fortress, 1995)

When Grief Breaks Your Heart, James Moore (Abingdon Press, 1994)

It Hurts to Lose a Special Person, Amy Mumford (Cook Communications Ministries, 1982)

Grief, Haddon Robinson (Discovery House, 1996)

You're Never Alone, Marie Shropshire (Harvest House, 1996)

Grace Disguised, G. Sittser (Zondervan, 1996)

Grief for a Season, Mildred Tengbom (Bethany House, 1989)

Mourning Into Dancing, Walter Wangerin (Zondervan, 1992)

Good Grief, Granger Westberg (Augsburg/Fortress, 1979)

E

ENVIRONMENT

Purpose
To enhance the learning environment and to design a setting for teaching or dramatizing the story of Esther

Preparation
- Paper
- Pencils
- Large cardboard boxes, large sheets of cardboard, or rolls of mural paper or fabric
- Utility scissors and mat knife
- Chalk
- Tempera paint
- Large brushes
- Duct tape
- Bible dictionaries, encyclopedias, or other reference books with historical and pictorial information about Persia

Procedure
Children, and adults as well, will love to act out the story of Queen Esther. Portray the story of Purim by writing your own script or describe the action with role play. Puppet shows are a perfect way to retell the favorite story. Check drama sources from public libraries or religious publications for ready-made scripts.

Whether the dramatic production is grand or small, the setting will enhance the storytelling. Create simple backgrounds by working cooperatively; arrange for groups to research and fabricate important scenes. Study pictures in reference materials to learn about appropriate buildings, scenery, and furnishings.

Sketch diagrams on paper first, then use chalk to redraw plans directly on the background material. Backdrops could include palace views, banquet settings, and courtyard sites. Paint the scenes on the paper, cardboard, or fabric; then attach to the back of the stage area or include as part of a classroom arrangement.

Design freestanding pieces to create the proper surroundings. Paint different views on each side of an appliance box. If large boxes are not available, join two or three sheets of cardboard with duct tape. Fold cardboard into three sections to form a backdrop that stands on its own. To change scenes, merely turn the box or cardboard "kiosk."

Large, fabric, banner-like panels are effective for depicting scenes. Sketch plans with pencil, then use tempera or fabric paints to complete the setting. Hang the banners from rods or clip panels along a clothesline rope. For easy storage, just roll up the scenery!

Make tall columns from cardboard or use large rolls from fabric stores or carpet suppliers. Add to the environment by including Persian-type rugs, drapery swags, mosaics, and brass ornamental items. Search through reference books for other ideas to enhance the surroundings for the story of Esther.

Creating a rich visual environment will bring the story to life, will provide lasting impressions, and will promote understanding of another time and culture.

F
FOODS

Purpose
To use food as a teaching tool to explore the events of the story of Esther

Preparation
- Materials vary with activity selected

Procedure
Food—in the form of fasts, feasts, and festivals—is a focus throughout the story of Esther. As the book begins, Xerxes hosts a 180-day banquet for officials from the 127 provinces that he rules. As that event concludes, another begins as the king throws a party for all the people in the citadel of Susa. At the same time, Queen Vashti entertains the women of the palace. Later in the story, when Esther risks her life to appeal to the king on behalf of the Jewish people, she invites Xerxes and Haman to banquets on two consecutive nights. In great contrast to feasting, the Jewish people—including Esther and Mordecai—spend time fasting and praying to empower Esther to accomplish her dangerous task. Finally, the story ends with the Jewish people celebrating a great festival, Purim, at which traditional and symbolic foods are served. Explore the story of Esther by experiencing foods related to the events.

FASTS
Fasting—abstaining from food and water—is a spiritual discipline. It is a tangible way of opening one's life to God. Fasting makes prayer a whole-body act. In the Bible there are many examples of fasting for spiritual reasons. The Old and New Testaments include stories of people who fasted for the sake of their relationship with God. Esther, Mordecai, and all of the Jewish people fasted as a way to empower Esther to approach the king to ask him to spare the lives of the Jews.

Explain the concept of fasting and note that this is one way to remind people of their dependence on God.

FEASTS
Esther probably enjoyed feasting on the products of Persia at the numerous banquets held in the palace. She may have enjoyed dates grown on the trees in the orchard, mutton from the sheep in the flock, or wine pressed from the grapes in the vineyard. Prepare a party and serve foods enjoyed by the people of Persia, the modern-day country of Iran.

HERBED YOGURT SOUP

Preparation
- 2 quarts plain yogurt
- ½ cup raisins
- ⅔ cup fresh cucumber, peeled and grated
- 1 medium onion, finely diced
- 1 tablespoon fresh dill, crushed
- Several springs fresh mint, crushed
- 1 teaspoon salt
- ⅛ teaspoon pepper

Procedure
Combine ingredients. Stir well and refrigerate several hours. Serve with pita bread.

PITA BREAD

Preparation
- 1 tablespoon active dry yeast (1 package)
- 2 cups warm water
- 1 tablespoon oil
- 6 cups flour
- 2 teaspoons salt

Procedure
Combine yeast and water in a large bowl, stirring occasionally for about 5 minutes until yeast is dissolved. Stir in oil, flour, and salt. Knead on lightly floured board until smooth and satiny. Place in greased bowl, turning greased side up. Cover and let rise about 45 minutes. Return to floured board and cut into twelve pieces. Shape into slightly flattened balls. Cover and let rest 20 minutes. Keep dough pieces covered at all times when not working with them to keep dough from drying out.

Preheat oven to 450 degrees. Heat cookie sheets, as it is important to place dough on heated sheets. Carefully roll rounds of dough into 6-inch circles, turning a quarter turn with each roll. Take care not to stretch, puncture, or crease dough. Place four rounds on hot cookie sheet. Bake 3–4 minutes until puffed and set. Turn over with spatula and brown 2 minutes more. Remove from sheet with hot pad or turner, leaving sheet in oven to stay hot while rolling next batch. Place bread rounds on cloth and cover with another cloth while cooling to keep pita soft. To serve, slit pita and fill as desired.

SKEWERED GROUND MEAT

Preparation
- 1 pound ground meat—beef, lamb, or turkey
- 1 onion, finely minced or grated
- 1 egg, beaten
- ¼ cup bread crumbs
- ¼ cup parsley leaves, finely minced
- ½ teaspoon salt
- Pepper to taste
- ½ teaspoon cinnamon

Procedure

Combine all ingredients. Wet hands in water and knead mixture thoroughly. Cover and refrigerate two hours. Divide mixture into six parts. Dampen hands and pat mixture around six skewers into long, flattened patties, about 1½ inches wide and 4–5 inches long. Grill or broil in oven until browned and cooked through, about 10–12 minutes. Serve with pita bread or brown rice.

FESTIVALS

Hamantaschen are cookies served at every Purim Festival. Some people say that the triangular shape of the pastry resembles the three-cornered hat worn by Haman when he was chief advisor to King Xerxes; others think that the word means "Haman's ears." Follow the recipe provided and sample this symbolic treat.

HAMANTASCHEN

Preparation

- 1 cup sugar
- ½ cup vegetable oil
- 3 large eggs
- Grated rind of 1 lemon
- ½ teaspoon vanilla
- 3 cups flour
- 2 teaspoons baking powder
- 2 cups of any berry jam

Procedure

In a large bowl, mix the first five ingredients together until they are blended well. Add flour and baking powder. Stir to form dough. Cover and chill for three hours. Roll the dough into the shape of a ball; cut ball in half. Roll out each half ⅛ inch thick on a lightly floured surface. Cut into 3 inch circles with a cookie cutter or a glass. Spoon 1 teaspoon filling in the center of each circle. Fold dough over the filling and pinch edges to form a triangle.

Place cookies 1 inch apart on greased cookie sheet. Bake 12–15 minutes, or until golden, in a preheated 375-degree oven. Makes approximately forty cookies.

G

GEOGRAPHY

Purpose
To locate and describe the country of Persia, the setting of the book of Esther

Preparation
- Bible atlas and current atlas
- Reference books with information and pictures about Persia and Iran
- Newspapers
- News magazines
- Transparency sheets
- Transparency markers

Procedure
Persia was the name of the country where Queen Esther lived. The great Persian Empire was established after the Medes and Persians defeated the Babylonians in the sixth century B.C. The Persian king, Cyrus, permitted the exiled Jews to return to Jerusalem to rebuild the walls of the city. Many of the Jews, however, remained in Persia because of family and jobs. One of these people was Esther.

All of the events in the book of Esther take place in Shushan (Susa), one of the capital cities of the Persian Empire. Xerxes was the king over lands reaching from India to Ethiopia. Persia encompassed the Iranian plateau, located between the Caspian Sea and the Armenian ranges on the north and the Persian Gulf on the south. The region is bounded on the west by the Tigris Valley and on the east by the Indus Valley. Archaeologists have uncovered ruins of the palace and fortress at Susa, the winter home of Xerxes and Esther. This area is near the modern-day city of Ahvaz in Iran.

In a Bible atlas, find a map of the Persian Empire, then locate the city of Shushan (Susa). Use a current map or atlas to find the corresponding region in modern-day Iran. If the maps are similar in scale, place a transparency sheet over the modern map and trace the landmarks, such as rivers, mountain ranges, and boundaries. Indicate some of the major cities. Use a marker made for drawing on acetate sheets. If the maps are not the same scale, use a photocopier to reduce or enlarge to make them comparable.

Place the transparency over the Bible atlas map and notice the changes in place names and national borders. Learn about Iran today. Describe the climate and other physical characteristics of the area. Look through reference books and look at photos of Persian architecture, mosaics, sculptures, and metalwork.

Skim through current issues of news magazines or recent newspapers to find articles about Iran. What are the similarities to events during Esther's life as queen of Persia? What are the differences? Compare and contrast.

Reread the story of Esther keeping in mind all that has been learned about the geography of the Persian Empire.

H

HANGMAN

Purpose
To play a variety of games as an active way to retell Esther's story

Preparation
- Supplies vary with activity selected

Procedure
Games are a great way to teach Bible stories. They give information and reinforce learning while players are having fun. Adapt familiar games such as Hangman, Jeopardy, and To Tell the Truth to fit the story of Esther. Try the suggestions provided and have fun while learning.

HANGMAN

Hangman is an appropriate game to play when teaching a lesson on the life of Esther. Review the passages about the "hangman" Haman and remember that although he built the gallows to hang Mordecai, Haman was actually the person who was hanged on them.

In the game of Hangman, a player has a word in mind and puts down as many dashes on a piece of paper or a chalkboard as there are letters in the word. To adapt this game format to the lesson, use only words associated with the story of Esther. To begin the game, a letter is called by another player. A skillful player usually calls the vowels first. If the guess is correct, the writer must put the letter in all the spaces wherever it appears in the word. If the guess is wrong, the writer begins to draw the scaffold and man. The object is to draw the whole man before the word is guessed.

With a large group, divide into two teams. Use a chalkboard. One side chooses a word and tries to "hang" the other side.

JEOPARDY

Since the word *jeopardy* means risk—a predominant theme in the book of Esther—it is also a good game to use to teach lessons related to the life of this brave woman. In the game of Jeopardy, an answer is revealed and the question must be supplied. To prepare a Jeopardy game board, select five categories, such as Major Characters, Minor Characters, Quotes, Numbers, and Vocabulary. Mark five columns on a piece of posterboard—one for each classification. Write five questions for each division on separate index cards and indicate the point value on the back of each card—10, 20, 30, 40, and 50. If possible, use a different color index card for each of the five categories. Sample questions could include:

Major Characters
   A: This faithful Jew dressed in sackcloth and ashes to proclaim his sorrow.
   Q: Who is Mordecai?

Minor Characters
A: This royal woman refused to do the king's bidding.
Q: Who is Vashti?

Quotes
A: The person to whom the king said, "Now what is your petition? It will be given you."
Q: Who is Esther?

Numbers
A: The number of days Esther requested the Jews to pray and fast.
Q: What is three?

Vocabulary
A: The Jewish feast Purim is taken from the meaning of this Persian word.
B: What is *lots*?

Attach the index cards for each category in a vertical column under the corresponding heading. Be sure that the point value, rather than the answer, is displayed.

Inform the players that one answer at a time will be revealed. The first individual or team will have one minute to state the question. If they provide the correct question, they will be given the point value indicated on the card. If they cannot come up with the question, the other player or team will have a turn to attempt to answer it. Rotate teams after each question. The game ends when all questions are answered or when a predetermined number of points is reached.

TO TELL THE TRUTH

In a game of To Tell the Truth, three individuals claim to be the same person. In this case the three could represent Esther, Xerxes, Mordecai, or Haman. To begin the session, introduce three players who have prepared their parts in advance. Invite the three to introduce themselves by saying, "I am _____." After the introductions an emcee should read a brief biography of the character.

One player gives accurate answers, another provides semicorrect responses, and the third shares information that is obviously incorrect. Answers should be given in a random order. Ask a series of questions to help the students learn information about the story of Esther. Give the participants opportunities to ask questions as well.

Take a vote to establish the real person.

I

INTERCESSION

Purpose
To write prayers for others, using the story of Esther as a way to understand and to practice intercessory prayer

Preparation
- Bibles
- Paper
- Pencils

Procedure
To *intercede* literally means "to go in between." An *intercessor* is someone who prays on behalf of someone else. Sometimes we might be tempted to think we are pleading another person's case with God, hoping that God might intervene to change the other person or the situation. The story of Esther gives a clearer picture of the meaning of intercessory prayer.

When Haman convinced the king to let him write a death sentence for all Jews, Mordecai began to let others know about the great danger by sacrificing his own personal comforts and communicating in a way that got everyone's attention, especially Queen Esther's. Mordecai speaks in faith to Esther, assuring her that God will send relief and deliverance in some way, but she may have been raised to prominence for "just such a time as this." Mordecai is a messenger for God and the Jewish nation, taking the message to Esther.

The deadly importance of the mission is not lost on Esther, but before acting, she requests further intercession on her behalf. Mordecai is to gather all the Jews, and they are to fast with her for three days before she goes to the king. God certainly does not need to be convinced to act. Mordecai implies that God has already been acting by raising Esther to such a position of prominence. So Esther, as an intercessor, is really sent by God to talk to the earthly king on behalf of God's people. What purpose is served, then, by the prayers and fasting of Esther, Mordecai, and the Jewish people if not to incite God to action?

The message of Esther is that true intercessory prayer is a power that changes the people involved. Mordecai receives power to get the queen's attention. Esther receives strength to face the king and wisdom to contrive a workable plan. The Jewish people receive courage to resist those who wish them harm. God's will is accomplished, and the chosen people are preserved. Their example teaches us that intercessory prayer is an act of the will, a decision to lay our lives before God, being open to take God's purpose as our purpose regardless of the risk involved.

The people in the story of Esther were willing to become intercessors because the outcome affected their nation, their families, and their own personal well-being. Whether leading youth or adults in a lesson on intercessory prayer, there will be topics they can think of that affect their nation, their families, and themselves. Invite each group member to choose a situation in any category for which they are willing to be God's intercessor. Have people write prayers for their concerns in their own words. Then challenge them to make a daily commitment to intercede with God.

They may want to pray their prayer for a specific length of time. They should choose a physical reminder as a call to prayer, like praying instead of eating at lunchtime or praying at every stoplight. Maybe people will even want to organize with others in the group to pray for the same concern in the same way. Don't neglect to set a time to follow up and see how God's will has been accomplished through changed people.

J

JEWISH HOLIDAYS

Purpose
To understand Jewish beliefs and customs by participating in celebrations of the Jewish holidays

Preparation
- Supplies vary with activity selected

Procedure
To help students, as well as an entire congregation, understand and appreciate Jewish religious beliefs and customs and to use these activities to explore and experience the meaning and the manner of the Jewish festivals. As each special day or season occurs, share information about it with the learners, or use this material to prepare a class or a series of learning centers based on the holiday celebrations.

Introduce the topic by explaining to the group that many Christian holidays are related to the life, death, and resurrection of Jesus Christ. Jewish holidays, however, recall events related to the interaction between God and the Jewish people. A few of the high holy days focus on the life of the individual Jew, but most recount historic times that the Jews experienced as a community. By celebrating the holiday festivals, Jewish children learn their people's history.

Jewish holidays may be classified in three categories: high holy days, pilgrimage festivals, and lesser or minor festivals. The high holy days, from Rosh Hashanah to Yom Kippur, are days of a purely spiritual nature. The pilgrimage festivals, including Passover and Sukkot, are days on which the Jews were required to make a pilgrimage to the temple in Jerusalem to bring an offering to God. These special days are significant for agricultural, historical, and spiritual reasons. Hanukkah and Purim are two of the lesser or minor festivals.

Since the Jewish calendar is a lunar calendar—based on the phases of the moon—the dates of the holidays vary from year to year. Consult a calendar for specific dates. Jewish holiday observances begin at sunset the day before the actual date and end at sunset on the date itself.

PURIM: FESTIVAL OF ESTHER; FEAST OF LOTS

Esther 2:1–9:5 records the story of Purim, which is sometimes called the Festival of Esther or the Feast of Lots. This is one of the merriest holidays of the Jewish year.

Ahasuerus, also known as Xerxes, was the king of Persia. The king asked for his queen, Vashti, to appear before the male guests he had been entertaining for many days. Vashti refused, so the king, fearing other women in the kingdom would follow her example, had her banished from the court.

After a beauty contest of sorts, Xerxes selected Esther, a beautiful Jewish woman, to be the new queen. Esther's relative Mordecai was a member of the king's court. He heard of an evil plot by the prime minister, Haman, to destroy all of the Jews. Mordecai persuaded Esther to go to the king to plead for mercy for their people. Esther was brave to go before the king, since he did not know she was Jewish and he had not summoned her according to custom.

Because of Esther's brave act, Haman's plot was discovered, he was killed, and the Jewish people were rescued. This holiday celebrates triumph over persecution. The name Purim comes from *Pur*, the lots cast by Haman to determine the date for the Jewish massacre. The festival features costumes, parades, skits, and merrymaking. As the story of Esther is read from a scroll called the *megillah*, listeners drown out the name of Haman by stamping, hissing, and using noisemakers.

Traditional symbols for Purim are special noisemakers called *groggers* and filled cookies called *hamantaschen,* in the shape of Haman's tri-cornered hat. Make groggers and masks to use as a reminder of this festive and fun holiday.

GROGGERS (Noisemakers)

Preparation
- Juice cans, empty and clean
- Cardboard
- Construction paper
- Duct tape
- Beans, buttons, or stones
- Scissors
- Markers
- Tongue depressors or craft sticks
- Pencils
- Glue

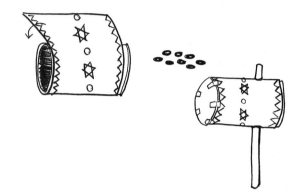

Procedure
Lightly roll a piece of colored paper around the can to determine the size; then mark and cut enough to cover the cylinder. Before attaching the paper, decorate with designs or symbols, then glue the covering to the can.

Place some beans, buttons, or stones in the can and cut a cardboard circle to fit the open end. Tape or glue the circle securely so it does not shake loose. Use a scissor blade to cut two slits opposite each other on the grogger. Push the stick through to form a handle. Fasten with tape or glue. Allow the glue to dry thoroughly, then try out the noisemaker.

PURIM MASKS

Preparation
- Half-masks, purchased or patterns
- Scissors
- Pencils
- Glue
- Tape
- Yarn
- Ribbon
- Feathers
- Paper scraps of fancy wrapping paper
- Sequins, buttons, "jewels"
- Cardstock
- Markers
- Stickers
- Hole punch

Procedure

Purim takes on a carnival atmosphere with all types of activities. Celebrations include masquerading as people such as Esther, Vashti, and Haman, or parading as colorful figures such as clowns. Create a fanciful mask and join in the holiday fun!

If using a mask pattern, trace and cut the shape from the cardstock. Be sure to cut the eye holes in the proper position. Place the mask on a working surface and add decorative trims in a pleasing arrangement. Glue the embellishments in place. Emphasize eyes with colorful marker outlines, but use care not to put anything near the opening that might injure eyes.

Punch small holes on each side of the mask for attaching ribbon or yarn. Tie on the festive mask and join in the Purim celebration!

PASSOVER: PESACH; FESTIVAL OF UNLEAVENED BREAD; FESTIVAL OF FREEDOM

Passover, celebrated on the fifteenth day of Nisan (March–April), is observed for seven or eight days. On the evening of the Passover, Jewish families gather around a festive dinner table to participate in the seder, which is both a meal and a worship service. Those present are given a *Haggadah*, a book which explains the seder. During the Passover, the Jews tell the story of the way in which God freed His people from slavery in Egypt. The tenth plague was that the firstborn in all Egypt was to die on an appointed night. If the doorpost was marked with the blood of a lamb, the firstborn of that house was spared. Moses instructed the Israelites to sacrifice a lamb, paint some of its blood on the doorposts of their homes, and prepare bread for their journey. Since they left so quickly, the bread did not have time to rise, thus unleavened bread is symbolic of the Passover. At the Red Sea, the large nation of slaves faced the obstacle of crossing the body of water. When Moses took his rod and held it over the water, a great miracle happened. The water spread apart so the people could pass on dry land. As the Egyptians came up behind, Moses again stretched his rod over the water. The waters returned and the Egyptians were drowned in the sea. The Israelites were free to leave Egypt. Passover commemorates this exodus.

To explain the events of Passover, special foods adorn a seder plate and are eaten during the ceremony. Four questions, which guide the telling of the historic event, are asked by the children. Remember Passover by asking the four questions and by creating a seder plate. If possible, taste the actual foods too.

FOUR QUESTIONS

Preparation
- Index cards
- Pens

Procedure

On Passover, the seder meal begins when a child asks the question, "Why is this night different from all other nights?" Through foods, games, songs, stories, and rituals, four questions are answered and the story of the deliverance of the Jewish people is shared. Write each of these four questions on a separate index card. Read each question to a different person and ask him or her to tell the answer. Learn about the events of Passover through these statements that have been used for thousands of years. The four question are:

1. Why do we eat only matzoh tonight? [The Israelites left Egypt so quickly that the bread they were preparing for their journey did not have time to rise.]
2. Why do we eat bitter herbs on Pesach night? [They are reminders of the suffering the Israelites endured as slaves in Egypt.]
3. Why do we dip the herbs twice tonight? [We dip once for tears of sorrow and once for a sign of hope.]
4. Why do we dine with special ceremony tonight? [We remember struggle and celebrate freedom.]

SEDER PLATE

Preparation
- Paper plates
- Markers
- Scissors
- Glue
- Magazines

Procedure
During Passover, symbolic foods placed on a seder plate are used to explain the story of the exodus of the Jewish people from their slavery in Egypt. Remember this important story by making paper seder plates. Read about or review each symbolic food and draw it onto a paper plate or cut a picture of the item from used magazines and glue it in place. Retell the story by talking about each element of the seder meal. If possible, taste some of the special foods. Symbolic foods include:

- Parsley—green like springtime; symbol of new life; salt water—tears of the Israelites during slavery
- Egg—symbol of life itself
- Watercress or horseradish—bitter, like slavery
- Matzoh—flat bread that did not have time to rise
- Charoset—apples and nut paste that symbolizes the mortar used in brick-making in Egypt
- Roasted bone—lamb sacrificed in Egypt

SHABUOTH: FEAST OF WEEKS; PENTECOST
The springtime festival of Shabuoth is also known as the Feast of Weeks and Pentecost. This holiday comes seven weeks after Pesach, or Passover, and it highlights God's gift of the Law and the firstfruits of the harvest. In Bible times, bread was baked from the grain of the spring harvest and was given as an offering at the temple in Jerusalem. The first lambs and kids were offered as gifts of thanksgiving to God.

Jewish people everywhere celebrate Shabuoth by decorating their homes with flowers and leafy branches to commemorate the firstfruits of the land. Create a branch with "blossoms" to add color to the holiday season.

FLOWERING BRANCH

Preparation
- Bare branches
- Small fluted paper cups for minimuffins or candy
- Glue
- Shallow containers for glue
- Markers
- Pencils

Procedure
Select a nicely shaped branch to decorate. Separate the fluted paper cups and pour glue into shallow containers. Choose only one color or pick several pastel shades of the paper cups for blossoms. In order to form flowers, pinch and twist the centers of the paper cups so the blossom will hold its shape. Dip the

ESTHER: Ideas A–Z Series

twisted end into the glue and attach it to the branch. Continue until the entire branch is covered with colorful blossoms.

Older children may enjoy using markers of a similar color to outline the edge of the paper. When the blossoms are formed, they will have interesting two-toned petals. Display the branches in a worship area, as a table decoration, or as part of a bulletin board arrangement.

TEN COMMANDMENT PARAPHRASE

Preparation
- Bibles
- Pencils
- Paper
- Markers
- Posterboard
- Rulers
- Bible dictionary
- Erasers

Procedure
Shabuoth is also known as the holiday of the giving of the Torah. This is the celebration thanking God for the Bible, or Torah, and for the Ten Commandments. It is during this season that many Jewish families begin teaching young children the Torah. Some synagogues have confirmation ceremonies for young people who have completed Jewish studies.

The Bible readings for Shabuoth, Exodus 19:21 and Deuteronomy 1:11, emphasize the presentation of the Law and the covenant with God. Read the Ten Commandments in several translations of the Bible, look up unfamiliar words, then paraphrase God's guides for living. Discuss the meaning of each commandment. Rewrite the laws into commonly used words. When the list is complete, copy the rules onto the posterboard. Use the ruler and pencil to make light guidelines for even lettering. Neatly color the letters and add drawings to help explain the rules. Use care to erase the pencil lines. Compare lists with others in the class and display for all to share.

ROSH HASHANAH: JEWISH NEW YEAR
The Jewish New Year, Rosh Hashanah, is observed according to the lunar calendar in either September or October. This holiday is a time of reflection, repentance, and prayers, when people take a serious look at the past year. Worshippers gather to pray with families and friends at the synagogue. The sound of the shofar, or ram's-horn trumpet, calls people to obey God's laws and reminds them to be kinder and better in the new year.

APPLES AND HONEY

Preparation
- Apples
- Cutting board
- Knife or special tool that slices and cores apples
- Honey
- Spoons
- Small paper plates
- Small paper cups

- Pencils
- Wet paper towels
- Napkins

Procedure

There is a spirit of hope for the new year and faith in God's forgiveness, which is symbolized throughout the holiday period by eating apples dipped in honey. A special prayer is said for this food: "May it be Thy will, O Lord, our God, to grant us a year that is good and sweet."

Memorize the Rosh Hashanah blessing and then eat a snack of apple slices dipped in honey. Read and recite the blessing several times then look away and try to remember the words. Repeat until the prayer is memorized. The words may be printed around the outside edge of a small paper plate.

Wash hands and apples before preparing the snack. Demonstrate the proper way to use the knife or the apple-slicing tool. Young children should have apple pieces prepared by an adult. Cut the apples into eighths and discard the seeds, stems, and core. Spoon a little honey into the paper cup. Pass out napkins and have wet towels handy to clean sticky fingers.

Think about last year and then discuss ways to make the new year "good and sweet." Say the prayer and enjoy the snack.

GREETING CARDS

Preparation
- Cardstock or construction paper
- Markers
- Patterns, pictures, or stickers of Jewish New Year symbols (shofar, six-pointed star, apple, honeybee, challah, Book of Life)
- Scissors
- Glue
- Pencils
- Calendar
- Envelopes
- Stamps
- Trims

Procedure

A popular custom for Rosh Hashanah is the exchanging of greeting cards filled with good wishes for the new year. A typical greeting, "May you be written into the Book of Life for a good year," refers to Jewish lore. Jews believe the Book of Life has a list of everyone's good and bad deeds. They believe that during the high holy days, God opens the book so people can correct the wrongs they committed during the year.

Fashion a greeting card to send to a Jewish friend or to serve as a reminder of hope for the new year. Fold the paper or cardstock to form a card. Use the patterns, pictures, stickers, markers, and various decorative trims to create holiday cards. On the inside write: "Happy New Year" or "May you be inscribed for a good year!"

Since the date for Rosh Hashanah varies each year, check a current calendar for the correct month and days. Complete the cards and place them in stamped, addressed envelopes. If class members do not have Jewish friends to receive the greetings, check with local nursing homes or retirement communities.

YOM KIPPUR: DAY OF ATONEMENT

Yom Kippur, the most solemn day in the Jewish year, is the tenth day after Rosh Hashanah. Observed in the Fall, it is a day of prayer and total fasting from sunset to sunset. Jewish people spend the ten days between Rosh Hashanah and Yom Kippur repenting of their sins. People ask for forgiveness from anyone they may have hurt. Jews believe they can only ask for God's forgiveness after they have asked for people's.

Yom Kippur, like all other Jewish holidays, begins in the evening. In the synagogue the people spend much time in prayer asking God for forgiveness. The Bible story of the prophet Jonah is read since it illustrates the need to ask for forgiveness.

Learn more about the holiday of Yom Kippur by reading and illustrating the story of Jonah and also by writing a poem on the theme of forgiveness.

JONAH'S STORY

Preparation
- Acetate transparencies
- Overhead projector
- Screen
- Bibles
- Permanent markers

Procedure
Introduce the story of Jonah by briefly reviewing the content and summarizing the theme. Assign portions of the passage to individuals or small groups and instruct them to illustrate these sections on acetate transparencies. The story may be organized in the following way:

- God calls Jonah to preach to the people of Nineveh.
- Jonah runs away from God and takes a boat to Tarshish.
- God creates a big storm and the boat begins to sink.
- The sailors throw Jonah overboard.
- A whale swallows Jonah and he lives inside of the great fish for three days.
- God hears Jonah's prayers and causes the whale to spit Jonah out on dry ground.
- Jonah asks for God's forgiveness.
- Jonah obeys God and goes to Nineveh to preach to the people.

Provide Bibles and tell the people to read the verses that pertain to the section of the story that they are to draw. If freehand drawing is not an option for the group, find coloring pages or Bible storybook illustrations of the Jonah account. Trace or thermafax them and color the pictures. Project the depictions at the appropriate places in the story.

FORGIVENESS POETRY

Preparation
- Paper
- Pens or markers

Procedure
Write an acrostic poem that focuses on the subject of forgiveness. Write the word *forgiveness* down the left side of a piece of paper. Use it as an outline and write a descriptive word associated with the theme of

forgiveness from each of its letters. For example: f—forget; o—others; r—reconciliation, and so forth. Compile a book of forgiveness poems contributed by many people.

SUKKOT: FEAST OF TABERNACLES; FESTIVAL OF BOOTHS

The fall harvest holiday, Sukkot, is also known as the Feast of Tabernacles or Festival of Booths. This time of thanksgiving comes eight days after Yom Kippur, the Day of Atonement. Simple tabernacles or booths are built to commemorate the shelters used by Jews traveling with Moses to the Promised Land.

The booths are framelike structures made of wood and cloth with branches loosely covering the roof so the stars and sun can shine through the leaves. Many families celebrate Sukkot by eating and sleeping in their sukkah during the holiday week.

Flowers, fruits, and vegetables decorate the booth as well as paper chains and other handmade items. Birds are favorite ornaments used for sukkah decorations. Fashion a sukkah and a colorful bird to add to the festive atmosphere of Sukkot.

SUKKAH

Preparation
- Shoe boxes
- Glue
- Pencils
- Construction paper scraps
- Small pine branches
- Scissors
- Rulers
- Markers
- Clear tape

Procedure
Remove the lid from a shoe box and set it aside. Place the box on one side with the bottom facing away from the worker. Use the pencil and ruler to mark lines for an opening in each end of the box. Cut carefully so the corners remain intact to keep the structure strong. Use paper scraps to cover the shoe box for a more woodlike appearance. Arrange the pine boughs across the top and glue or tape them in place. Decorate the inside of the sukkah with paper flowers and tiny chains made from construction paper scraps. Some artists will want to fashion miniature fruits and vegetables to create a harvest look. Add simple furniture and figures for a diorama.

BIRD

Preparation
- Plastic eggs (any size)
- Tissue paper, vivid colors
- Feathers
- Ribbon
- Paper scraps
- Scissors
- Glue
- String
- Miscellaneous trims: sequins, beads

ESTHER: Ideas A–Z Series

- Containers and brushes for glue
- Table cover
- Wing pattern

Procedure

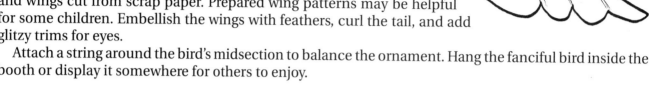

Select an egg and cut a piece of tissue paper large enough to cover the shape. Brush glue over the surface of the egg and gently press paper onto the damp glue covering the plastic surface. Glue on a beak, tail, and wings cut from scrap paper. Prepared wing patterns may be helpful for some children. Embellish the wings with feathers, curl the tail, and add glitzy trims for eyes.

Attach a string around the bird's midsection to balance the ornament. Hang the fanciful bird inside the booth or display it somewhere for others to enjoy.

HANUKKAH: FESTIVAL OF LIGHTS; FESTIVAL OF DEDICATION

Chanukah, Chanukkah, Hanukah, Hanukkah—regardless of the spelling, this Jewish festival celebrated on the twenty-fifth day of the Hebrew month of Kislev, generally December, commemorates the recapture of the temple and the miracle of the oil. Over two thousand years ago when the Syrian-Greek Antiochus Epiphanes ruled Judea, he prohibited the practice of Judaism under threat of death. He claimed the sacred temple and turned it into a place of pagan worship. Under the leadership of Mattathias, a respected leader of the people, and his five sons and many followers, the Jewish people organized a revolt. One of the sons, Judah Maccabee, led the army for three years and managed to regain Jerusalem. When they reclaimed the temple they looked for oil for the menorah, the eight-branched candelabrum that was always to be burning, and found a small amount, enough for one day. Miraculously, the oil lasted for eight full days, giving the priests time to prepare oil to keep the eternal flame lit without interruption. Therefore, Hanukkah is celebrated for eight days, one for each day the oil burned.

Jewish families today observe Hanukkah by gathering around the menorah and lighting one candle each night. Special prayers are said over the lights, thanking God for miracles in ancient and modern times. Presents are given and games involving a four-sided top called a dreidel are played. Foods made with oil, the symbol of the miracle, are eaten. These include special potato pancakes, named *latkes*, and fat jelly doughnuts. Engage the participants in exploring Hanukkah traditions by making a puppet to use to retell the victory story and by creating dreidels to play the traditional game.

JUDAH MACCABEE PUPPET

Preparation
- Small paper bags
- Construction paper
- Scissors
- Glue

Procedure

Turn a paper bag into a puppet representing Judah Maccabee and use it to tell the story of the victory of Hanukkah. Use the flap of the bag as the face of the puppet. To form the face, glue colored shapes to look like hair, eyes, nose, and moustache. Glue a small strip of red paper under the flap to be the mouth. Cut out arms and paste them on the sides of the bag. Glue a sword in one hand and a shield in the other. Make paper bag puppets of other Hanukkah characters and have a puppet show. Illustrate the story of the rededication of the temple and the miracle of the oil.

DREIDEL

Preparation
- Manila file folders
- Rulers
- Pencils
- Markers
- Illustration of Hebrew letters
- Large needle
- Q-tips
- Glue

Procedure

A dreidel is a top, usually four-sided, with a Hebrew letter on each side—nun, gimel, hey, and shin—the first letter in the four Hebrew words meaning "A great miracle happened there."

Construct a dreidel by cutting a 2-inch square out of a manila file folder. Using a ruler, draw two diagonal lines across the square from corner to corner. Write one of the Hebrew letters in each section. Using a large needle, poke a hole in the center of the square where the lines intersect. Take the cotton off of one end of a Q-tip and insert the stick halfway through the hole. The side with the remaining cotton should be at the bottom, with the Hebrew letters facing up. Adjust the square so that it is perpendicular to the Q-tip. Squeeze drops of glue around the hole to hold the square in place. Practice spinning the dreidels on a flat surface.

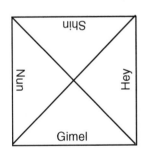
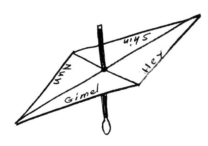

 Nun — Do nothing

Gimel — Take main pile

 Hey — Take half the main pile

Shin — Give half of your pile

HOW TO PLAY THE DREIDEL GAME

Divide the "treasure" (marbles, beans, or pennies) equally among the players sitting in the circle. Each player puts one treasure in the center of the circle; this becomes the main pile. The first player spins the dreidel and follows the directions above for the Hebrew letter that points up. Then the second player takes his or her turn, and so on. When a player loses his or her treasure, he or she is out of the game. The player left with the most treasure wins the game.

K

KEY VERSE

Purpose
To use a guided meditation as a way to reflect on the events and the key verse, Esther 4:14

Preparation
- Bible(s)
- Guided-meditation script
- Paper
- Pens

Procedure
Invite the participants to use a guided meditation as a way to reflect on the key verse of the book of Esther, 4:14. Look up the passage in the Bible and read the verse together: "For if you remain silent at this time, relief and deliverance for the Jews will arise from another place, but you and your father's family will perish. And who knows but that you have come to royal position for such a time as this?"

Use the script provided to help the students explore God's guidance and direction throughout Esther's experience and to apply the story to their personal situations.

Arrange the learners in a circle or in rows in such a way that each person can be seen by the leader. Invite everyone to close his or her eyes and relax. Read the meditation script or ad lib it from memory. As an alternative, record the script in advance and play it back for the group. Pause after every phrase or two so that the listeners have time to imagine what is being described.

SCRIPT

Take a moment to reflect on the events recorded in the book of Esther. *(pause)*

Imagine what it was like to feast with King Xerxes, *(pause)*

A beautifully decorated banquet hall—food of all kinds—in golden dishes, *(pause)*

All you could eat and drink for days at a time. *(pause)*

Imagine Vashti, the queen, being called to make an appearance—and refusing. *(pause)*

Imagine the anger of the king. *(pause)*

Picture Xerxes calling his advisors together to help him to decide what to do. *(pause)*

See how Vashti is banished from the king's presence. *(pause)*

Picture Esther summoned to the palace and prepared to meet the king. *(pause)*

See the delight on the king's face when he meets Esther. *(pause)*

Imagine Esther's place of prominence in the royal house. *(pause)*

See Esther telling the king how her cousin Mordecai discovered a plot to assassinate the king. *(pause)*

Watch the king's servants write Mordecai's good deed in the royal book of records. *(pause)*

See Mordecai refuse to bow down to Haman. *(pause)*

Imagine Haman plotting to kill Mordecai and all the Jews. *(pause)*

Picture Haman telling the king the terrible plan. *(pause)*

See Mordecai go into mourning, wearing sackcloth and ashes. *(pause)*

Listen to Mordecai tell Esther that the Jews are in danger. *(pause)*

Hear Mordecai challenge Esther with the words, "Do not think that because you are in the king's house you alone of all the Jews will escape. For if you remain silent at this time, relief and deliverance for the Jews will arise from another place, but you and your father's family will perish. And who knows but that you have come to royal position for such a time as this." *(pause)*

Imagine all the Jews of the city fasting and praying for Esther. *(pause)*

Watch Esther risk her life to go into the presence of the king. *(pause)*

See the king extend his royal scepter to her to spare her life. *(pause)*

Hear Esther invite the king and Haman to a banquet. *(pause)*

Imagine Haman's delight at being a guest of honor at Esther's banquet. *(pause)*

Watch Esther, Xerxes, and Haman feasting together. *(pause)*

Listen to the king ask Esther to tell him what she wants. *(pause)*

Hear Esther invite the men to a second banquet. *(pause)*

Reflect on Esther's request to the king to save her life. *(pause)*

Imagine the surprise on the king's face when he learns that Esther is a Jew. *(pause)*

Picture the king reviewing the royal records and remembering how Mordecai saved his life. *(pause)*

Imagine Haman's humiliation at being forced to honor Mordecai. *(pause)*

See Haman hanged and the Jews being given permission to arm themselves and defeat their enemies. *(pause)*

Picture Mordecai receiving his royal robes. *(pause)*

Pretend that you are part of the first Purim celebration. *(pause)*

Pause for a moment and look at your own life. *(pause)*

What circumstances have you found yourself in where God used you? *(pause)*

How did God use you in those circumstances? *(pause)*

Perhaps to help someone in need, perhaps to give a word of encouragement—*(pause)*

Perhaps even to save a life. *(pause)*

Stop to give thanks for those moments—and to acknowledge the One who put you there. *(pause)*

When you are ready, open your eyes and sit quietly in your place. *(pause)*

Following the meditation, invite those who wish to share their thoughts and feelings on the passage to do so. If the participants wish to write their reflections, rather than verbalize them, provide paper and pens or pencils for this purpose.

L

LOTS

Purpose
To explain the customs for celebrating the Festival of Lots, also called Purim, and to provide instructions for making holiday noisemakers, called "groggers"

Preparation
- Small containers such as juice cans, spice boxes, or match boxes
- Craft sticks
- Gesso or acrylic paint
- Paint brushes
- Scissors
- Glue
- Pebbles, dried beans, bottle caps, or buttons
- Paper plates or foil pie pans
- Stapler and staples
- Markers
- Rubber bands
- Six-pointed-star pattern
- Stickers
- Crepe-paper streamers
- Duct tape
- Hammer
- Nails
- Blocks of wood
- Sand paper
- Small tacks

Procedure
Purim, also known as the Feast of Lots or the Festival of Esther, is a carnival-like holiday with something for everyone—a public reading of Esther's story, drama and melodrama, costumes and masks, music and noisy merrymaking, special foods and drinks. This festive celebration commemorates the deliverance of Persian Jews from persecution and death.

Purim comes from the Hebrew word *pur,* which means "lots." In ancient times, when making decisions sometimes people would cast "lots," or throw stones on the ground to see what patterns were formed. Casting lots depends on chance and is similar to a lottery or comparable to throwing dice. When Haman cast lots to decide on a date to attack the Jews and to send Mordecai to the gallows, he interpreted the numbers to mean the thirteenth of Adar.

When Esther informed the king of the evil plot, Xerxes ordered that Haman be hanged instead of Mordecai. The Jews escaped destruction and celebrated on the fourteenth day of Adar. The holiday begins at sundown on the thirteenth and continues the next day.

Festivities include parties, masquerades, parades, puppet plays, and parodies of Bible stories. There is a Purim feast complete with *hamantaschen,* traditional three-cornered pastries, for dessert. The pastries are supposed to represent the shape of Haman's hat. They have jam or poppy-seed filling.

Another tradition of Purim is recorded in Esther 9:22. The Jews were informed that they would "observe the days as days of feasting and joy and giving presents of food to one another and gifts to the poor." It is customary to donate food or money to at least two poor people. Special food gifts—usually sweet treats and fruit baskets—are given to friends. Among the favorite Purim activities for children are helping to prepare the food gifts, called *shalakhmones,* and decorating food containers. Sometimes children wear costumes as they deliver the gifts.

The main event of Purim is the reading of the megillah, or the Scroll of Esther. During the reading of the megillah, listeners are required to "blot out" the name of Haman. Each time the reader says Haman's name, everyone stomps, shouts, and makes as much noise as possible. Children especially enjoy shaking noisemakers called *groggers.* Instructions follow for groggers made from recycled or available materials.

For very young children, create a noisemaker from paper plates or small aluminum foil pie pans. Fold the plate or pan in half and place a few large buttons or bottle caps inside and staple to fasten the edges. Place staples close together so buttons or caps do not fall out while the noisemaker is being used.

Decorate the noisemaker with paint or stickers. For a handle, push a craft stick between the plate edges near the fold. Secure it with glue or tape. An option is to omit the handle and hold on to the corner of the folded plate when shaking the grogger. Add crepe-paper streamers for a bit of color.

As another option, an empty juice container provides a base for a really noisy grogger. The easiest type to work with is the cardboard can that holds frozen juice. Wash and dry the can. If the top is fastened with a plastic pull strip, save the lid to reattach to the opened end; otherwise, cut a circle of cardboard to fit over the opening.

Cover the can with gesso or other acrylic paint. When the paint dries, decorate with a picture of Haman's three-cornered hat, six-pointed stars, or any colorful motif. The adult leader will need to use a scissor blade or a knife to make two small slits opposite each other on the cylinder. Slide the craft stick through both slits to form a handle. Wrap rubber bands around the two ends of the stick. Push the wrapped bands up to the can, on both sides, to secure the handle.

Put a few buttons, beans, or pebbles in the can; try rice or lentils for a less raucous sound! Cover the open end with the original lid or a cardboard circle. Use duct tape or strong glue to attach the lid. Allow the glue to dry.

For version three, make a cap rattle to add to the clamor! Flatten metal bottle caps with a hammer or use metal lids from juice cans. Pierce a hole through the center of several lids or caps using a hammer and a long slender nail. Slide the caps onto the nail, then pound the nail into a block of wood. The caps should be able to move back and forth freely along the shaft of the nail. Shake the rattle at the sound of Haman's name.

For version four, make a few sets of "whisper" blocks by tacking sandpaper to one side of two wooden blocks. Rub the blocks together to produce a "whisper," or rustling sound.

Consider constructing noisemakers from other containers such as spice tins, matchboxes, or small gift boxes. Add sleigh bells, wooden dowels, plus pots and pans to the collection of noisemakers. Be sure to secure handles, lids, and any added trims so the gadget can withstand vigorous shaking. Find some earplugs, then join in the noisy celebration!

MEGILLAH

Purpose
To understand the basic story line of the megillah, which is the book of Esther, and to learn several methods to make scrolls for presenting the story

Preparation
- Materials needed will be determined by the type and size of scroll selected.
- Paper: rolls for adding machines, shelf paper, table covering, or butcher paper
- Rods: toothpicks, skewers, pencils, dowels, cardboard tubes from giftwrap, large tubes from fabric or carpet stores
- Scissors
- Rulers or yardsticks
- Colored pencils
- Erasers
- Markers, fine or wide tips
- Tape
- Glue
- Ribbon
- Bible
- Outline or story of Esther

Procedure
The book of Esther, or Scroll of Esther, is usually referred to as the megillah. The word *megillah* is the Hebrew word for "scroll," which reminds us that early writings of the Bible were written on rolls of paper. The megillah is usually written on parchment and sometimes has a wooden winder on one end.

The scroll is unrolled and read as part of the observance of the festival of Purim. To understand the origin of the holiday, participants should read the book of Esther. For younger children, read to them about Esther from a Bible storybook or invite a storyteller to describe the events.

A favorite activity of Purim is to draw pictures, record phrases, or write out parts of the story in the form of a scroll.

Use the following directions to make a scroll. The smaller sizes are suitable for individuals to make; larger ones can be made cooperatively by groups.

Cut narrow adding machine tape into a strip approximately 12 inches long. Draw important scenes from the megillah using fine-tipped markers or colored pencils. Glue or tape each end of the strip to a toothpick. Roll the two ends to meet in the middle of the paper strip or begin at one end and roll the paper all the way to the other end, following the traditional form for the megillah. Use wider strips of paper and skewers or pencils for another type of small scroll. Tie a ribbon around the rolled paper to finish the scroll.

Larger scrolls can be fashioned in the same way with longer sticks or with long cardboard tubes. Rolls of shelf paper or butcher paper work well for drawing and lettering. Use a ruler to mark light pencil guidelines for any words or phrases. Print the captions along the guidelines under scenes from the story or between pictures.

Main portions of the megillah are listed below:

King Xerxes has a big party in the palace.
Queen Vashti refuses to attend.
Xerxes looks for a replacement for Vashti.
Esther is chosen to be queen of Persia.
Haman plans to destroy the Jews.
Mordecai discovers Haman's wicked plan.
Mordecai asks Esther to tell the king about the plot.
Esther has dinner with Haman and King Xerxes.
Esther tells the king of Haman's plan and that she is Jewish.
Haman is hanged on the gallows intended for Mordecai.
Mordecai is honored by the king.
The Jewish people are saved.
The Feast of Purim is established as a holiday for Jewish people to celebrate deliverance.

Look over the scrolls to review what happened to Queen Esther. Make plans to visit another class to share this story of courage and faithfulness.

N
NOTES

Purpose
To use music to teach the story of Esther

Preparation
- Music to selected songs
- Accompaniment

Procedure
Use notes—musical notes, that is—to tell the story of Esther. Take a familiar tune, add new words, and create a song. Try the two examples provided. One combines the music of the children's song "B-I-N-G-O" with verses about the key people in the book of Esther. The other blends contemporary words of challenge with the traditional tune "O for a Thousand Tongues to Sing." In addition to these sample songs, pick a favorite melody and write new words to fit the lesson.

E-ST-H-E-R

[Tune: B-I-N-G-O]

Let's sing about the people in
the Bible book of Esther
P-EO-P-L-E
P-EO-P-L-E
P-EO-P-L-E
Those in the book of Esther.

There was a king who ruled the land
And Xerxes was his name-o
X-ER-X-E-S
X-ER-X-E-S
X-ER-X-E-S
And Xerxes was his name-o

There as a Queen who disobeyed
And Vashti was her name-o
V-AS-H-T-I
V-AS-H-T-I
V-AS-H-T-I
And Vashti was her name-o

There was a girl who trusted God
And Esther was her name-o
E-ST-H-E-R
E-ST-H-E-R

E-ST-H-E-R
And Esther was her name-o

There was an evil, wicked man
And Haman was his name-o
H-A-M-A-N
H-A-M-A-N
H-A-M-A-N
And Haman was his name-o

There was a man who love the Lord,
Mordecai was his name-o
M-OR-DE-CA-I
M-OR-DE-CA-I
M-OR-DE-CA-I
Mordecai was his name-o

When Esther risked her life in faith
God saved the Jewish people
S-A-V-E-D
S-A-V-E-D
S-A-V-E-D
God saved the Jewish people.

GOD, COULD IT BE?

    Text: John A. Dalles, 1996
    Tune: *Azmon*
    Meter: C.M. (8.6.8.6.)

God, could it be that we are called
to bring the light of morn
into the shadow-lands of life?
Perhaps for this we're born!

God, could it be that we are called
to comfort those who mourn
and dry the tears of those who cry?
Perhaps for this we're born!

God, could it be that we are called
to mend a life that's torn
with hopeful, helpful, healing hands?
Perhaps for this we're born.

God, could it be that we are called
to give rest to the worn,
and guide the ones who've lost their way?
Perhaps for this we're born!

    The words of this hymn may be reprinted without special permission for one-time use only, provided that the following acknowledgement is included: From *Ideas A-Z: Esther*. Words © 1996 John A. Dalles. Used by permission.

OBEDIENCE

Purpose
To learn the value of setting boundaries to follow by creating a dictionary of English and Hebrew words related to the story of Esther

Preparation
- Bibles
- Dictionaries and an English-Hebrew dictionary, if possible
- Paper
- Pencils
- Stapler or hole punch and yarn

Procedure
To create a dictionary is to define, to set limits on interpretation, so that words may be used and understood by all to create shared meaning. Similarly, to live a life of faith requires accepting limits on our behavior so that we may share God's blessing. The process of submitting to those limits we call "obedience." Esther is a story of obedience: Esther's obedience to Mordecai, her obedience to the king's court, and ultimately, her obedience to God's call on her life.

To help participants see the necessity for agreeing to certain limits on life and to deepen their understanding of the story of Esther, work together to create a dictionary of words related to the story. Make it clear that, to be useful, every language must set agreed-upon definitions of words and determine rules for using those words so that people can communicate. Invite participants to find key words and words that they don't know in the book of Esther. Also make a list of related Hebrew words. For example:

Purim (POOR-im) *n.* the Jewish holiday that celebrates the rescue of the Persian Jews from Haman's plot; also the Persian word for "dice" or "lots," which was the method Haman used to determine the date for the Jews' extermination. Since that date became their day of deliverance, the name Purim was given to the celebration.

Grogger (GRAHG-er) *n.* a rattle or noisemaker like those used at the Purim celebration.

Megillat Ester (meh-GE-latt es-TAIR) *n.* the Scroll of Esther

Guide the selection of English words to include important concepts like *obedience, intercession,* and *petition,* and background terms like *sackcloth, signet ring,* or *gallows.* Let small groups work cooperatively to find definitions and discuss proper contexts for using their new vocabulary. Once they have the words alphabetized and defined, then provide paper and pencils or pens for their "dictionaries." Encourage creativity through illustrations, sentence examples, and word choices. Add decorated covers and staple, or punch dictionaries and bind them with yarn.

Be sure to make the point that to communicate well we must all obey certain laws about language, and to live well we must all obey God's laws about life.

P

PUPPETS

Purpose
To tell the story of Esther through a puppet play

Preparation
- Paper tubes
- Felt
- Yarn or fake fur
- Fabric scraps
- Scissors
- Glue
- Craft sticks or dowel rods

Procedure
What is a puppet? "Any inanimate shape or form given some identity and moved by a person before an audience to convey an idea or message becomes a puppet" (Roland Sylvester, *Teaching Bible Stories Effectively With Puppets* [St. Louis: Concordia, 1976].)

Puppetry is the art of bringing an inanimate object to "life" and communicating a thought, theme, or topic with it. Bring the book of Esther to life by making and using puppets. Instructions are supplied for constructing puppets from paper tubes, and a script—an artistic interpretation of the story—is provided as the basis of a performance.

To begin the project, determine the characters needed for the puppet show. The script "The Story of Purim" requires:

Xerxes, the king
Vashti, the queen
Hegai, the king's servant
Haman, the prime minister
Mordecai, an old man
Esther, a young woman

To create the characters, turn paper tubes of any size into puppets. Use a small tube, such as a toilet paper roll or a paper towel tube, or a large tube, like a wrapping paper roll or a carpet or fabric tube.

Form the puppet face by cutting a piece of felt and gluing it to the top one-third of the tube. Make facial features from felt scraps and glue them in place. Yarn or fake fur becomes hair and should be attached to the top of the tube.

Adapted by permission from Eleanor Boylan, *Holiday Plays for Puppets or People* (Rowayton, Conn.: New Plays, 1974).

Glue a piece of felt around the remainder of the tube to serve as the undergarment. Layers of fabric in contrasting or complementary colors can be added as overgarments. Make arms from strips of cloth or felt and glue them to the sides of the tube. If felt is not available, use construction paper instead. The facial features may be drawn on with marker. Substitute tissue paper for fabric to form the outer garments.

Apply a craft stick to the inside back of the tube to serve as the rod by which the puppet is operated.

THE STORY OF PURIM

[Xerxes enters. Bows and addresses audience]

NARRATOR
    Once long ago, when the Jewish people were captives in the land of Persia, a great and powerful king ruled there. His name was Xerxes.

XERXES
    No one is greater than I
    All bow to my command;
    Everyone fears my wrath
    In this great Persian land.

[Bows again. Exits]
[Vashti enters. Bows to audience]

NARRATOR
    But the queen, whose name was Vashti, did not always obey the king.

VASHTI
    The queen of Persia am I,
    And I will not obey!
    Though you'll see as the story unfolds
    For my folly I'll soon pay.

[Bows. Exits]
[Hegai enters. Bows to audience]

NARRATOR
    The king had a faithful servant named Hegai, who carried out the king's commands.

HEGAI
    I serve the king
    As his trusted man.
    To find a new queen,
    I have a plan.

[Bows. Exits]
[Haman enters. Bows to audience]

NARRATOR
    The king had a prime minister named Haman, a wicked, ambitious man, who hated the Jewish people.

HAMAN
    I am Haman, full of hate!
    There are many things I abominate
    Especially the Persian Jews —
    I'd destroy them all if I could choose!

[Bows. Exits.]
[Mordecai enters. Bows to audience]

NARRATOR
> Also living at the court was a just man named Mordecai. He was a Jew and much respected by the king.

MORDECAI
> My name is Mordecai, I bow
> To Israel's God, to no one else
> Though haughty Haman tries to make
> Me bow before his heathen self!

[Bows. Exits]
[Esther enters. Bows to audience]

NARRATOR
> There was one more person about to become a member of this court, but as yet she was only a simple Hebrew woman named Esther. She was a relative of Mordecai and very beautiful.

ESTHER
> I am Esther, a simple maid,
> My uncle has taught me, and I have prayed
> That all my life I may serve and love
> The God of Israel above.

[Bows. Exits]

NARRATOR
> And so, our story of Purim begins!

[Vashti enters, followed by Hegai]

VASHTI
> I refuse! I flatly refuse!

HEGAI
> The king will be angry, Queen Vashti. He expressly wishes you to attend his banquet to display your beauty and your jewels.

VASHTI
> I detest being ordered to attend these banquets so all may stare at me. I'll not go.

HEGAI
> You are firm in this resolve?

VASHTI
> Firm!

HEGAI
> Then in the name of the king, I pronounce his sentence upon you. Queen Vashti, you are banished from court!

VASHTI
> Banished?

HEGAI
> This is the king's command. Be gone!

[Vashti exits with bowed head]
[The king enters]

XERXES
>Hegai, where is the queen?

HEGAI
>She refused to appear before you, Sir, and I carried out your sentence of banishment.

XERXES
>So, I have no queen?!? She must be replaced. But, by whom?

HEGAI
>Oh, this is a matter of grave importance, Sir. Let me give it serious thought.

[Pause]

>I have it! Your Majesty, decree that all the fairest young women in your land be brought to the court to pass in procession before you. You will then be able to judge their beauty and pick the fairest.

XERXES
>Excellent idea! Send out the decree!

[Xerxes and Hegai exit]

NARRATOR
>So all the fairest young women in the land of Persia came to the court of Xerxes, and on the morning of the procession, the king came out onto his balcony. Mordecai watched from the courtyard.

[Xerxes and Hegai enter to one side]

>Slowly the young women begin to walk by, bowing low before the king.

XERXES
>There's a lovely creature. See there—the young woman in yellow with the crimson veil.

HEGAI
>Do not choose hastily, Sir. Reserve your judgment until all have passed.

[Esther approaches]

NARRATOR
>Mordecai had his own candidate—his niece, Esther, and she had not yet passed before the king. But now she was approaching, and to Mordecai's joy, the king leaned far forward over the balcony, his eyes fixed on Esther.

XERXES
>Stop the procession! The young woman in blue! Her beauty outshines all the rest. She will be my queen! I will prepare to meet her.

[King exits, followed by Hegai. Mordecai bows his head in prayer]

MORDECAI
>Oh, God of Israel be thanked
>For you have made fair Esther queen.
>Her beauty will your glory show,
>though none must know her faith.

[He glances over his shoulder]

>No, none must know!

[Esther enters and approaches Mordecai]

ESTHER
>Uncle! I'm frightened!

MORDECAI
: No, no, child, do not be frightened. The King has done you a great honor. But do not tell him that you are a Jewish woman. Do you understand me, Esther? It is best that he not know this for the present. Be virtuous and true, child, and God will protect our people.

[Mordecai and Esther exit]

NARRATOR
: Time passed, and Esther reigned as Queen, most beloved by her husband and by all the people. But now Haman's hatred of the Jews grew out of all bounds and he determined to destroy them.

[The king and Haman enter]

HAMAN
: Your Majesty, I have discovered a rebellion among the people.

XERXES
: What?

HAMAN
: Oh yes, Sir! The Jewish people do not follow the king's laws or commandments.

XERXES
: The fiends.

HAMAN
: And do not consult Mordecai about this, I beg you, for he is himself a Jew and would only deny the plot to protect his people.

XERXES
: True . . . true . . . this could be true!

HAMAN
: Let me handle it, Sir. I will instruct your soldiers to fall upon these Hebrew traitors and slaughter them all.

XERXES
: Let it be done!

[Xerxes exits. Haman dances for joy]

HAMAN
: Ha! Ha! Hee! Hee!
My dreams have all come true!
At last I can extinguish every single Jew!
There'll be a slaughter—what a merry jest!
And Mordecai shall perish with the rest!

[Haman dances out]

NARRATOR
: And Haman cast lots to determine which would be the day of the slaughter. And the lot fell upon the thirteenth day of the twelfth month. But Mordecai, learning of this dreadful scheme, hurried to tell Esther.

[Mordecai and Esther enter]

MORDECAI
: Esther, my dear, we are in deadly danger!

ESTHER
: Danger?

MORDECAI
> Haman has invented a terrible story! He has told the king that the Jewish people are rebels who disobey the law.

ESTHER
> But how could the king believe such a lie?

MORDECAI
> I do not know, Esther, I do not know! But I do know that you must go to the king at once and beg mercy for our people.

ESTHER
> But, uncle—you know the rule in Persia. No one, not even the queen, may go into the king's presence unless sent for.

MORDECAI
> That is the chance you will have to take, my child. You have won the king's love, now you must trust the God of Israel to protect you.

[Mordecai exits. Esther bows in an attitude of prayer]

ESTHER
> Oh, God of Israel, I ask
> Your blessing on this dangerous task;
> I go to plead for all I cherish,
> And if I perish—I must perish.

[Exits]

NARRATOR
> And that evening, as the King sat on his throne, Esther came before him.

[Xerxes enters and sits on his throne]

XERXES
> What, Esther? You come before me unbidden, uninvited?

[Esther enters, bowing low]

ESTHER
> I come before you, Sir, because the need that brings me is so great I dare to risk your anger.

XERXES
> Well, Esther, you are my queen as well as my subject. Rise.

ESTHER
> I am your queen, Sir, but not your subject, for indeed, I am not a Persian woman, but a Hebrew.

XERXES
> Why are you telling me now?

ESTHER
> Because the Jews in Persia are in cruel danger, Your Majesty! They have been falsely accused by Haman of a plot against you.

XERXES
> Falsely?

ESTHER
: All my life I have lived among the Hebrew people. They are loyal to you, they serve you faithfully in this land, and most loyal of all is Mordecai—my uncle.

XERXES
: Your uncle?

ESTHER
: Only recently, Sir, he prevented a true plot to murder you. It was written in the Book of Records. Look through the book where all the deeds of your kingdom are recorded. Only read, Sir, I beg of you—read—and spare my people!

[Bows in an attitude of prayer]
[Xerxes exits. Returns quickly]

XERXES
: It is Haman who shall die! Send for him, Esther—and for Mordecai, too!

[Esther exits. King paces]

So Haman thinks he's fooled us all,
That we believe his wicked plot,
He thinks he's very clever but
I now shall prove that he is not!

[Haman enters, followed by Mordecai]

HAMAN
: You wanted to see me, Sir?

XERXES
: I do. I want to ask you both the same question. Mordecai, suppose I were to discover traitors in my land who were plotting to murder me. What action would you suggest I take?

MORDECAI
: Well, your majesty, knowing your wisdom and your justice I'd suggest that you give the accused a fair trial, then deal with them according to the outcome.

XERXES
: I see. Haman, what would you suggest?

HAMAN
: Well, I'd suggest no trial, no justice, and no mercy! I'd set up a gallows in the courtyard and execute 'em all!

XERXES
: Quite so! Mordecai, suppose on the other hand I were to learn that someone in my court had uncovered such a plot and prevented it. How would I thank this person?

MORDECAI
: Oh, Sir, the king's gratitude would be enough thanks for anyone.

XERXES
: Haman?

HAMAN
: Well, I think that such a person should be clothed with a royal robe and escorted through the land that all might know what the king owes to him.

XERXES
> Splendid. Let a royal robe be brought and placed upon—Mordecai!

HAMAN
> What???

XERXES
> And a gallows erected in the courtyard upon which Haman will die! Wretch! You have betrayed me and the loyal Hebrew people of Persia!

[Haman slinks out]

> Let Queen Esther be sent to me!

MORDECAI
> Your Majesty, may the Lord of Israel bless and protect you. My people have been saved.

[Esther enters]

ESTHER
> Sir?

XERXES
> Esther, my queen. I will leave it to you to inform the Jewish people that they have been delivered from Haman's wicked scheme.

ESTHER
> Sir, my heart is filled with joy and gratitude. And may it please you to hear how I will tell the joyful tidings? I have learned that Haman cast lots to determine the day of the slaughter. In Hebrew, the word *Pur* means to cast lots. I will declare a day of rejoicing called "Purim," which for all time will be a day when the Jewish people will thank God for His goodness.

MORDECAI
> And a day when we will always remember the beautiful and good Queen Esther.

[Xerxes, Esther, and Mordecai exit]

QUESTIONS

Purpose
To develop open-ended questions as a guide to study the book of Esther

Preparation
- Bibles
- Paper
- Pencils

Procedure
Educational experts suggest that we learn best what we must teach others. Often students—whether in the school or the church classroom—feel that their job is to learn how to answer questions, rather than learn how to ask them. Use the story of Esther as a way to instruct readers about the importance of questioning skills.

First, explain the difference between closed-ended and open-ended questions. A closed-ended question can be answered yes or no or other one-word responses. An open-ended question requires the respondent to elaborate and give more information. To check to see whether the concept is understood look at some questions asked in the book of Esther. Look at the question put to Mordecai in chapter 3, verse 3, "Why do you disobey the king's command?" Discuss why it is an open-ended question and what Mordecai's response must have been, based on verse 4. Ask participants to speculate what open-ended question might have been asked Mordecai as a follow-up to his answer. A suggestion might be, "Why must Jews not bow down to Haman?" See if they understand the biblical reasons for Mordecai refusing to bow to a human.

Another open-ended question is modeled by the king in chapter 5, verse 3, "What is your request?" Discuss possible reasons why Esther avoided answering that question and instead issued an invitation. Another good example of an open-ended question is found in chapter 6, verse 6, "What should be done for the man the king delights to honor?" Haman, of course, misinterprets and answers as though he were "the man."

Once all seem to understand the idea of open-ended questions, explain that they are going to create open-ended questions about the book of Esther to help others think about the story and its meaning. Practice creating one or two questions together first. Point out that a question like "What is the setting of the story?" really only gives us one answer: "Persia." But a question like, "What is going on in the king's court as the story begins?" requires much more information and understanding to answer. They can also use imaginative questions like, "What questions might Queen Esther have been asking herself when she heard Mordecai's news?"

Consider dividing the story into segments and assigning each part to different small groups. They should come up with open-ended questions about their segments and challenge the other groups to answer. Each group should write its own example of a good answer to its question(s). Compile questions to create a study guide over each part of the story and to share with other church classes.

If time permits, create closed-ended questions to use as answers in a Jeopardy game. Compare the difference in information gathered from closed-ended and open-ended questions. Another option might be to consult a Serendipity Bible and compare its open-ended questions to your own.

R

RHYTHM STORY

Purpose
To use a rhythm story to teach the account of Esther

Preparation
- Rhythm-story script

Procedure
Use rhythm and rhyme to tell the story of Esther. This method involves the learners in the process and assures that the lesson will be memorable and meaningful.

The words of the rhythm story may be written on newsprint, on a chalkboard, or may simply be emphasized with the voice.

To tell the story, have the participants sit or stand facing the leader. Begin by establishing the clapping pattern, one clap on the knees and one clap of the hands. Practice the beat several times. Say the first line of the story to this rhythm and tell the group to echo, or repeat, it back. Communicate the entire story in this manner. Maintain the established rhythm throughout the activity.

RHYTHM STORY

When Xerxes was king of Persia
He held a banquet for all around.
There were many months of feasting;
It was the biggest party in town.

To please the men at the party
He called Queen Vashti to dance.
But he banned her from the kingdom
When she said, "There's not a chance!"

The king was sad and lonely
So his officials had a plan.
"We'll find the most beautiful woman
To be queen for this powerful man."

When Mordecai learned of the contest
He brought his relative Esther to be
the queen of all of Persia.
The king said, "She pleases me!"

An evil man named Haman
Had a very wicked plan:
"Let's kill all the Jews in Persia
We don't want them in our land."

When Mordecai got this message,
He tore his clothes with a cry.
He begged and pleaded with Esther:
"Tell the king or we all will die."

Esther was a Jew, in secret;
Now her life was on the line.
So she invited Xerxes and Haman,
They said, "Yes! We'll come and dine!"

At the banquet she asked a favor,
"Come to dinner tomorrow night."
She told the king of Haman's plot,
"Save us from this terrible plight."

Now the king was filled with anger—
Who would dare such a wicked plan?
Esther pointed her finger at Haman:
"Your official is the evil man."

Then Haman was hanged on the gallows
That he had built to kill a Jew.
Mordecai was made prime minister
In power he was number two.

God spared the Jewish people.
Esther and Mordecai led the way.
Jews celebrate the Feast of Purim
To commemorate this happy day.

S

STORYTELLING

Purpose
To involve all participants in the telling of the story of Esther

Preparation
- Script
- Posterboard
- Markers
- Scissors
- Costumes (optional)

Advance Preparation
- Prepare four posterboard signs to use while telling the story of Esther. Print words on the placard for each character as follows:

King Xerxes—"May he live forever!"
Mordecai—"Yay!"
Esther—"Ah-h-h-h-h!"
Haman—"Boo!" or "Hiss!"

Procedure
Esther involved the Jewish people in her efforts by having them pray with and for her before she risked a visit to the king. She wisely understood that we remember those events in which we invest ourselves. Audience participation stories are always a popular way to involve everyone in the telling of a tale. Acting out the story of Esther is still an important part of Purim celebrations.

To help present-day readers invest themselves in the story of Esther, divide listeners into four groups. Then select a person from each group to represent one of the four main characters from the story. These representatives will hold up signs whenever they hear their character's name mentioned in the story. At that time everyone in their section will perform the action and make the sound for that character.

Instruct the Xerxes group to bow from the waist with arms extended forward and say, "May he live forever!" every time they hear the king's name. Likewise, Mordecai's group should clasp their hands above their heads and shout, "Yay!" Queen Esther's group should place prayerful hands alongside their cheeks and say, "Ah-h-h-h!" Finally, Haman's group should cup their hands around their mouths and shout, "Boo!" or "Hiss!" Dress leaders or others in simple costumes to portray the characters, if desired.

Begin reading the story, pausing each time a character's name is mentioned so everyone can salute, cheer, sigh, or boo.

STORY SCRIPT
Once upon a time in a far-off land called Persia, there lived a powerful king named **Xerxes**. In his kingdom also lived a Jewish man named **Mordecai** who was raising his orphaned niece, the beautiful **Esther**, as though she were his own daughter.

One day, **King Xerxes** decided to look for a beautiful woman to be his new queen. **Mordecai** permitted

Esther to be considered among all the beautiful women of the kingdom, but she was not to tell anyone that she was a Jew.

From all the beautiful women of the kingdom, **King Xerxes** selected **Esther** to be his queen. **Mordecai**, in his job just outside the palace, kept a close eye on what happened to **Esther**. She continued to be obedient to **Mordecai**, and **Esther** told no one that she was Jewish.

Now **King Xerxes** had a chief assistant named **Haman**, who was so proud of his position in the kingdom that he made everyone bow down to him when he passed. But **Mordecai** refused to bow down to **Haman**. **Mordecai** bowed only before God.

When **Haman** learned that **Mordecai** refused to bow down because **Mordecai** was a Jew, **Haman** convinced **King Xerxes** to let him kill all the Jewish people in the Persian Empire.

Haman cast lots to determine a date to kill all the Jewish people. When **Mordecai** learned of **Haman's** evil plot, he sent word to **Queen Esther** asking her to help her people. **Esther** was afraid to go in to **King Xerxes** to let him know the problem because if she went to the throne room without an invitation she might be killed.

But **Esther** found her courage when **Mordecai** reminded her that God might have brought her to be queen just so that she could save her people. **Esther** asked **Mordecai** to help her defeat **Haman's** evil plan by praying for three days with all the Jewish people. Then she would go to **King Xerxes**.

After three days of fasting and prayer, **Queen Esther** gathered her courage and approached **King Xerxes'** throne even though she had not been invited. **King Xerxes** looked on his beautiful queen and promised to grant her anything she wanted. **Queen Esther** invited **King Xerxes** and **Haman** to a banquet. **Haman** was proud to have been invited by **Queen Esther**. Neither **Haman** nor **King Xerxes** knew that **Queen Esther** was Jewish or that **Mordecai** was her uncle. After the success of the banquet, **Queen Esther** invited **King Xerxes** and **Haman** to return the next night for a second banquet.

At the second banquet, **Queen Esther** told **King Xerxes** of **Haman's** wicked plan to kill all the Jews. **King Xerxes** was so angry with **Haman** that he had **Haman** hanged on the gallows that **Haman** had built to kill **Mordecai**. All the Jewish people were saved because of the courage of **Queen Esther** and her uncle, **Mordecai**.

Still today, the Jewish people celebrate the Feast of Purim to remember the day that their lives were saved by the beautiful and brave **Queen Esther**.

T

TRIPS

Purpose
To use field trips as learning experiences to explore the story of Esther

Preparation
- Research and material vary with activity selected

Procedure
Pretend that you are an elementary school student. Recall the Bible story of Esther, perhaps the part about the Feast of Lots. Would you rather hear about festivities or go to a Purim carnival to experience some of the sights, sounds, and smells firsthand?

As a middle school student you have great curiosity about other countries and cultures. There's going to be an ethnic festival in town featuring food, music, dances, and crafts from many lands. Would you prefer watching a movie about various places in the world or participating in an event exploring some of them?

Imagine that you are in high school. Think about Christ's commission to share your faith, through word and deed, with all people of the world, near and far. What would make a greater impression on your life: reading stories about ministry or going on a mission trip to meet needs and to make a difference?

In these situations—and many others—information, insight, and inspiration not only would be imparted, but also would have a lasting impact on the young people who participate in an experience. It's reported that people retain a small percentage of what they hear, a greater percentage of what they see, and the highest percentage of what they do. One way to help children apply and appreciate what they learn in Sunday school—or any other Sunday or midweek ministry—is to take them on a field trip. But before you go, know the purpose, the plan, and the preparation needed.

PURPOSE
There are many reasons for taking a field trip. A few reasons are to have fun, to find facts, and to learn with a fresh approach. Serving, socializing, and sightseeing are others. Select one or several of these purposes as the focus of the outing. The reasons should help the participants increase their understanding of Bible truths.

PLAN
Picking the place is the first priority when planning a field trip. Survey the community—and beyond—to determine locations that can provide meaningful experiences for the learners. Obtain information about various places by reading literature, making phone calls, and visiting in person. Keeping in mind the purpose of the trip, select a site. Choose a date and set a time. Field trips may be held during the regular Sunday or midweek session; however, another day may need to be selected to provide more time for the excursion.

Depending on the time of year and the theme to be communicated by the event, there are numerous places to go on a field trip to learn about the life and story of Esther. Consider these suggestions: natural history museums (especially a section on Persia), art galleries (biblical, Jewish, and Persian collections), libraries, synagogues (especially during a service), Hebrew day schools, Purim carnivals, bookstores, resource centers, and gift shops.

PREPARE

After finding a site and finalizing arrangements with the contact person, preparations must be made for the outing. Communicate information about the field trip to students and parents verbally and in writing. Recruit several adults to serve as chaperons. The number required will be determined by the ages of the children in the group. Enlist the help of the adult supervisors and others to provide rides. Additional transportation options are to reserve a church van or bus or reconfirm schedules and rates for public transportation such as buses or trains.

Produce permission slips and send them home with instructions for completing and returning them before the time of the event. Include information regarding the food, money, or materials required for each person.

Increase the effectiveness of the field trip and the enjoyment of the participants by preparing the learners in advance. Help the group know what to expect and what is expected of them by sharing information on the purpose and plans for the outing. Answer questions that arise.

Prepare a guide for the children to use during the field trip or develop a list of questions to answer during the visit.

PROCEED

As the participants arrive, be sure that everyone has turned in a permission slip and that each person has the required materials and money. Distribute name tags to the youth and adults, make introductions, and arrange people in their respective groups. On the way to the field trip destination, provide additional information about the place and restate the purpose of the outing. Affirm good behavior in positive ways, and review rules and expectations for the event. Encourage the young people to look, listen, and learn! Be sure to designate the departure time and location, especially if small groups will proceed on their own for part of the time.

PROCESS

Processing is as important as planning, preparing, and proceeding. If an activity sheet was used during the outing, review it with the group. Encourage discussion and questions. Provide an opportunity for the children to respond to the event by writing, drawing, acting, or singing. Depending on the age-group involved, an evaluation form could be completed by each participant. As a class or as individuals, write thank you notes to the contact person, chaperons, and others who helped with the trip. Be sure to provide resources for further exploration into the theme or topic.

U

UNIQUENESS

Purpose
To involve adults in reflecting on their own spiritual journeys in relation to the story of Esther

Preparation
- Paper
- Pencils
- Newsprint (optional)
- Overhead projector (optional)
- Markers (optional)

Procedure
One of the unique features of the book of Esther is that in its original version God's name does not appear in any form. Also, while remnants of all the other books in the Hebrew Bible have been identified as part of the Dead Sea Scrolls, no scroll of Esther has been found at the Dead Sea. This apparently concerned the devout Jews who lived in the Essene community so much that they questioned putting Esther in the biblical canon. Early leaders of the Christian community questioned this as well. Yet any thoughtful reading of the book of Esther reveals God's presence quietly working behind the scenes to save the Jewish people. One way to appreciate just how many times God can be seen at work in Esther's life would be to map out the story, charting what happens at each twist and turn of the plot.

After reading the book of Esther, invite people to brainstorm the significant events that occur in this story. Many instances could be included: Esther is chosen queen, Mordecai persuades Esther to intercede for the Jewish people, and the king and Haman attend Esther's banquets. Encourage participants to depict the turning points graphically as though creating a map of Esther's life. This could be done on newsprint or with an overhead projector in a large group or by small groups creating their own maps. Have participants then explain how God is seen in each significant moment.

To reflect on the unique spiritual journey of each person in the group, have participants create maps of the significant events in their own lives. Assure them that they will share with others only what they choose, but they should try to chart the twists and turns of their own life stories—events such as births, marriages, moves, job changes, and so forth. After the maps are created, challenge them to see where God has been at work providing help, strength, and courage when it was needed. Then have each find a partner and choose one significant event from the map to share with the other person. As time permits, let volunteers share important stories with the whole group, or encourage participants to write about one meaningful moment they selected. Close by reminding everyone that each of us is a unique chapter in the story of faith, brought into being by God, like Esther, for such a time as this.

V
VERSE

Purpose
To view the significance of Esther 4:14 as a personal challenge to discover God's purpose for our own lives

Preparation
- Bibles
- Pizza rounds or circles cut from cardboard
- Posterboard
- Pencils
- Markers
- Rulers
- Compass
- Knife or razor cutter (for leader—optional)

Procedure
"Who knows? Perhaps you have come to the kingdom for just such a time as this" Esther 4:14 (NRSV).

With these words Mordecai pricks the heart of Esther to accept that God had a plan for her life that was of greater importance than her own personal survival. Esther 4:14 can impact the lives of those who read and understand its challenge today.

Most of us will never be royalty; few of us are raised to highly visible positions of prominence or fame. Yet each of us has been given a life to share with the world in whatever sphere of influence each enjoys. Is it possible that God's will is not accomplished more often because we don't hear Mordecai's challenge to choose to be God's person for "just such a time as this"?

Offer participants an opportunity to memorize this important verse from the story of Esther by creating a sundial to remind them of the words and meaning behind them.

As a part of this activity, tell the group a sundial is one way of measuring time. Be sure to discuss how the sundial works, marking time by the shadow cast from the sun. Explain that our lives are made up of moments, each one possibly filled with opportunity to be of use to God. Like Esther, we must be ready to accept that God is working in the situations of our lives and wants our cooperation.

Use a small pizza round or a circle cut from cardboard to form the face of the sundial. With a compass, draw the biggest circle possible; then set the compass to draw a smaller circle about an inch inside the larger one. Mark off the edge of the outer circle in twelve equal spaces to represent the hours of the day. Make a dot above each mark to indicate the point at which the hours will change. Make marks for quarter hours, too, if desired. Use Roman numerals to label each of the hours in the space between the two circles.

Cut a V-shaped triangle from poster board. Fold down one side of the V to make a flat edge down the center of the triangle shape. If working with older youth or adults, a slit may be cut in the cardboard from below the numeral XII to the center point of the circle. Slide the triangle into the slot as far as the crease, fold along the crease, and glue the half underneath to the bottom of the sundial. If time or age-level does not permit this process, simply glue the flat edge to the face of the sundial in the position just below the numeral XII.

ESTHER: Ideas A–Z Series

Decorate the face of the sundial with the words from Esther 4:14, "Perhaps you have come to the kingdom for just such a time as this."

Challenge participants to memorize this verse. Point out that the V can stand for the verse they memorize, the numeral five on the clock, or for the victory we are sure to win if we work with God when the time is right.

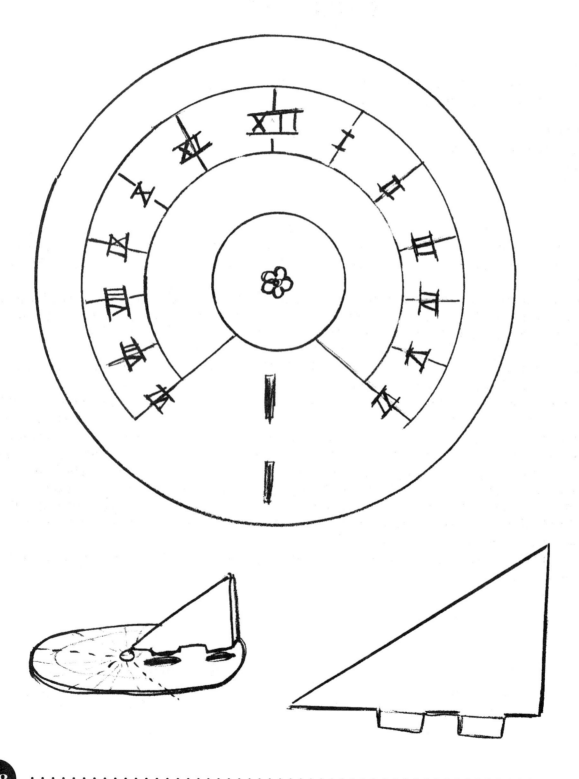

ESTHER: Ideas A–Z Series

WRITING

Purpose
To challenge readers to consider the choices Esther made by writing alternative choices in a choose-your-own-adventure story of Esther

Preparation
- Bibles or children's Bibles
- Paper
- Pencils

Procedure
Putting ideas in writing gives them power. When Haman asked for permission to annihilate the Jews, he requested that the king issue a decree. The king had his scribes write the edict in the script and language of every province. It is the copy of this written document that Mordecai sent to persuade Esther to act on behalf of her people.

Writing in response to the story of Esther can be a powerful tool for understanding the significance of human choices. As the Bible story of Esther unfolds, many people are faced with decisions that impact the story's outcome. Obviously, the most important choice occurs when Esther decided to go to the king on behalf of her people with the words, "If I perish, I perish." Yet readers or listeners may miss the significance of other human choices that affect the book of Esther's development and outcome. Challenge participants to put themselves in the story by participating as writers.

Many people should be familiar with a choose-your-own-adventure style of storytelling. If needed, explain briefly that in such stories writers pause at critical moments and let readers have a choice in how the plot progresses. If one choice occurs, the resulting story will have one outcome; if the opposite occurs, the plot will develop quite differently. Brainstorm critical moments in the story, starting from the beginning when Vashti refuses to go to the king. List as many of these decisive moments as possible. Then allow pairs of writers to select one of the critical moments and write an alternative choice and result.

If desired, collect all the written options and compile them so that the entire story can be read with the different twists of plot based on readers' choices. More simply, have writers read aloud their versions of how the characters' different choices might affect the story's outcome.

Close the reading or sharing time with a final discussion question, "What if the story of Esther had never been written?"

X

XERXES

Purpose
To match husbands and wives from the Old Testament in addition to Xerxes, king of Persia, and Esther, his Jewish queen

Preparation
- Bibles
- Scrap paper
- Construction paper, assorted colors
- Pencils
- Heart pattern
- Scissors
- Bulletin board
- White paper or fabric to cover bulletin board
- Stapler and staples
- Straight pins or tacks
- Large zip-type plastic bags (or baskets)
- Fine-point black marker
- Letter patterns or precut letters
- List of names and references for husbands and wives in the Old Testament

Procedure
Xerxes I was the son of Darius I and became king of Persia in 485 B.C. He was considered to be a great builder and a wise administrator. Xerxes is also called Ahasuerus, who is mentioned in the books of Ezra, Esther, and Daniel. According to the book of Esther, the king deposed his wife, Vashti, and planned to replace her. Xerxes selected Esther, a beautiful Jewish woman to be his queen.

Besides Xerxes and Esther, there are many other couples mentioned in the Old Testament. Design a bulletin board display with a matching game to acquaint students with husbands and wives in the Bible.

Before class begins, cover the bulletin board space with white paper or fabric. Prepare letters for the caption: Bible Couples. In smaller letters, add the subtitle: Matching Game. Center the caption, then add a border to frame the display. Trace and cut one heart for each pair. Use a variety of colors. Write the names of one important pair on each heart, with the husband's name on the left and the wife's name on the right. Cut the hearts in half, then place all of the women's names in one plastic bag and the men's in the other. Pin the bags to the bulletin board and instruct the players to work together to match the halves. Post a list of Scripture clues to find out who's who. Encourage the students to read the passages to learn about the important couples.

Place a small table or TV tray near the display so players can spread out the halves as they attempt to match couples. Matching colors will help find some of the pairs. To make the game more challenging, use one color of paper for all of the hearts! Pin matched pieces to the bulletin board.

At the end of the session, return the hearts or heart halves to the plastic bags so another group can play when the class meets again. Allow the learners to play the game until they know which Bible people belong together. After two or three class periods, pin the matched hearts around the caption. Another way to vary the game would be to write a Bible reference on each heart. Direct the players to look up the Scripture clues to discover some of the husbands and wives. Each time a combination is discovered, write the names on the heart and pin it to the bulletin board.

BIBLE COUPLES	SCRIPTURE CLUES
Adam and Eve	Genesis 3:20
Abraham and Sarah	Genesis 17:15
Isaac and Rebekah	Genesis 24:67
Jacob and Rachel	Genesis 29:18
Joseph and Asenath	Genesis 41:45
Amram and Jochebed	Exodus 2:1–2; 6:20
Moses and Zipporah	Exodus 2:21
Elimelech and Naomi	Ruth 1:2
Boaz and Ruth	Ruth 4:13
Elkanah and Hannah	1 Samuel 1:1–2
Saul and Ahinoam	1 Samuel 14:50
Nabal and Abigail	1 Samuel 25:3
David and Bathsheba	2 Samuel 11:27
Ahab and Jezebel	1 Kings 16:30–31
Hosea and Gomer	Hosea 1:2–3
Xerxes and Esther	Esther 2:16
Haman and Zeresh	Esther 5:10

Y
YEAR

Purpose
To learn about the Jewish calendar and to compare the Jewish way of counting time with the Gregorian and Christian calendars

Preparation
- Paper
- Pencils
- Rulers
- Pizza rounds or 8-inch circles cut from posterboard
- Soft erasers
- Scissors
- Glue sticks
- Fine-point markers
- Colored pencils
- Brass paper fasteners
- Black paper strips
- Patterns for dial and circle
- Photocopies of calendar diagram
- Reference books with calendar information

Advance Preparation
Ahead of time, make an overhead transparency or copies of the circular diagram shown. Use a photocopier to enlarge the circular calendar diagram to fit 8 ½-by-11 inch copy paper. The information should include the Hebrew months and a corresponding modern calendar as well as the Christian seasons. Make a copy for each learner. Prepare circle and dial patterns.

Procedure
Calendars are guides for us to measure and record the passage of time. The very earliest calendars were designed to coincide with natural seasons so people would know when to plant and when to harvest. According to tradition, the Hebrew calendar began with the Creation, 3,760 years before the start of the Christian era and the calendar we use. To find out what year it is on the Hebrew calendar, add 3,760 to the current year of the familiar calendar.

The Gregorian calendar, which is used in many countries, traces the earth's 365-day journey around the sun. The Jewish calendar is different because it is based on the moon's phases; days for religious observances were determined by new moons, as well. A Jewish year, or twelve lunar cycles, totals only 354 days. Every few years an extra month is added around March, or the Jewish month of Adar. This calendar adjustment is known as Adar II, or Adar Sheni.

The Jewish month names are Nisan, Iyar, Sivan, Tammuz, Av, Elul, Tishri, Heshvan, Kislev, Tevet, Shevat,

Adar, and Adar Sheni. There are several spellings for some of the months because the Hebrew language is based on phonetics, the sounds of the syllables, not exact letter combinations. Another variation is that the Jewish year has two beginnings: Rosh Hashanah, in the month of Tishri, which indicates the completion of Creation and the birth of the world, and Passover, in the month of Nisan, which marks the birth of the Hebrew nation. The months in the story of Esther refer to the Nisan year. Some of the important holiday months are listed below:

Nisan	March/April	Pesach/Passover
Sivan	May/June	Shabouth/Pentecost
Tishri	September	Rosh Hashanah/New Year
	October	Yom Kippur/Day of Atonement
		Sukkot/Feast of Tabernacles
Adar	February/March	Purim/Festival of Lots

Study the circular diagram and locate the holiday seasons and corresponding months for both the Jewish and the Christian traditions.

Each participant should have a cardboard circle, a copy of the diagram, and scissors. Glue sticks, markers, and other supplies may be shared by the class members. Write the months, seasons, and holidays in the proper sections of each ring. Some children may prefer to write the information in pencil first, correct any mistakes, then trace over the words with a fine-point marker. When marker ink is dry, erase any pencil lines that show.

Cut out the calendar diagram and glue it to the cardboard. Trace the dial pattern onto one of the black strips of paper and cut out. Push the points of a brass paper fastener into the round end of the dial, then into the center of the calendar to join the pieces. For easier assembly, use a scissor point to pierce a small hole in the calendar and cardboard. Finish the calendar by coloring the sections for each of the Christian seasons; add other holiday symbols if there is room.

Advent and Lent—purple
Christmas and Easter—white
Epiphany—green/gold
Pentecost—red
Ordinary Time—green

In some traditions, blue is used for Advent and ordinary time may be called kingdomtide or late Pentecost. Use colors that follow the traditions of your church.

Turn the dial to the current month to see which Jewish month and Christian season correspond. Move the dial to indicate the new year on the Western calendar, the new school year, the beginning of a new planting season, and your birth month—which will mark the beginning of your personal new year. Find Adar, the month for the celebration of the Festival of Esther.

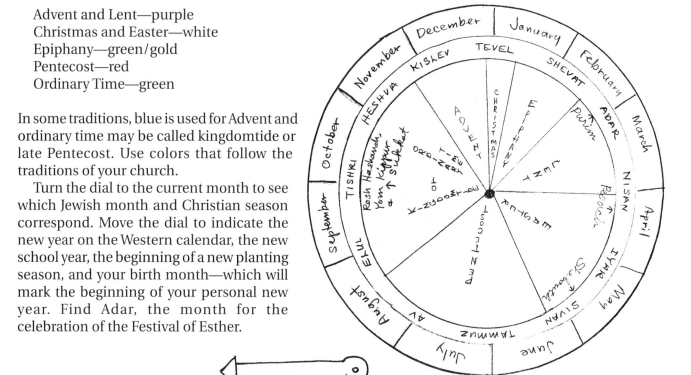

ESTHER: Ideas A–Z Series

Z

ZERESH PLUS

Purpose
To encourage critical thinking skills and to expand readers' perspectives by role-playing and asking questions between the characters in the story of Esther

Preparation
- Bibles
- Slips with individual character names and references
- Box to hold slips for drawing
- Paper
- Pencils
- Costumes (optional)

Procedure
The story of Esther has a large cast.

Major Characters
Xerxes (1:1)
Mordecai (2:5)
Esther (2:7)
Haman (3:1)

Minor Characters
Vashti (1:9)
Hegai (2:8–9)
Shaashgaz (2:14)
Bigthana (2:21)
Teresh (2:21)
Hathach (4:5–9)
Zeresh (5:10; 6:13)

Seven Eunichs (1:10)
Mehuman
Biztha
Harbona (7:9)
Bigtha
Abagtha
Zethar
Carcas

Seven Noble Advisors (1:14)
Carshena
Shethar
Admatha
Tarshish
Meres
Marsena
Memucan (also vv. 16–20)

Ten Sons of Haman (9:7–9)
Parshandatha
Dalphon
Aspatha
Poratha
Adalia
Aridatha
Parmashta
Arisai
Aridai
Vaizatha

Help participants appreciate that everyone has a point of view and plays a significant role in the unfolding of the plot by role-playing imagined questions among cast members. Zeresh, who seemed to know that Mordecai would be her husband's downfall, must have suffered greatly when all of her ten sons were killed. What questions might she ask of Mordecai or Esther if given the chance? Such imaginative speculation enlarges our perspective on a story and inspires divergent thinking and creativity. We also will remember the story and the people more vividly than when we simply read or memorize.

First, have each person choose one character by drawing a name at random. Be sure to cover all the major characters, adding minor and less-developed characters as numbers allow. Allow participants time to find references to the person whose name they drew. If time permits, have them write a few sentences describing the character's personality and attitude (they may have to read between the lines or use their imaginations based on the reference and other information provided in the story).

Next, collect the slips of paper from the first drawing and have participants choose a second time (have them return the name and draw again if they select their same character). This time they are to imagine what their original character would have to say to the second person whose name they drew. They should then write one or two open-ended questions for their first character to ask their second one.

Conclude by actually pairing the characters involved and role-playing the interview. Participants must respond as they think their character would, based on the information in the story. If an interviewee gets stuck allow some time for consultation of the others as "advisors" on how he or she should respond. Add costumes for interest, if desired. If possible, videotape the interviews to share with others.

As a follow-up activity, save the character descriptions written and use them for a game of Trivial Pursuit or Concentration.

RESOURCES

For Children

Books
dePaola, Tomie. *Queen Esther*. San Francisco: Harper & Row, 1986.
Lovett, Linda. *Esther (Book of Esther): A Bible Story to Color*. Norwalk, Conn.: C. R. Gibson, 1972.
Wolkstein, Diane. *Esther's Story*. New York: Morrow Junior Books, 1996.

Videos
Esther. The Children's Heroes of the Bible. Lutheran Church in America, 1988.
"Esther." *Animated Stories from the Bible*. Family Entertainment Network, 1992.
"Queen Esther." *Greatest Adventure: Stories from the Bible*. Hanna-Barbera, 1986.
"Queen Esther Saves Her People." *Kings and Prophets*. Children's Video Bible, no. 3. Oxford Vision, 1988.
"Story of Esther." *Greatest Heroes of the Bible*. Magnum, 1987.

For Adults
Bankson, Marjory Zoet. *Braided Streams: Esther and a Woman's Way of Growing*. San Diego, Calif.: LuraMedia, 1985.
Geiger, Lura Jane, and Pat Backman. *Braided Streams: Leader's Guide*. San Diego, Calif.: LuraMedia, 1986.
Osterman, Mary Jo. *1 Kings–Esther*. Journey through the Bible, vol. 5. Nashville, Tenn.: Cokesbury, 1995.
Vander Berg, Edward, and Robert Meyering. *1001 Persian Nights: A Reader's Theater of the Book of Esther*. Grand Rapids: CRC Publications, 1996.

Hymn Stories for Children

Help children discover the rich heritage of the Christian faith through these great resources.

Grades K-6

Phyllis Vos Wezeman and Anna L. Liechty have created a series of resource books that will introduce children to the stories behind the great hymns of the faith. Each book in the series centers around a specific topic and contains at least twenty-six hymn stories complete with suggested story narrations, Scripture references, and craft activities along with complete instructions, reproducible craft sheets, and materials list. Choose one or all in this six volume series for grades K–6. Great for use in children's church, Christian schools, Sunday school, Christian day school, or even at home.

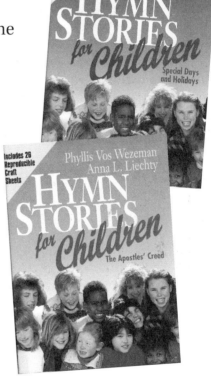

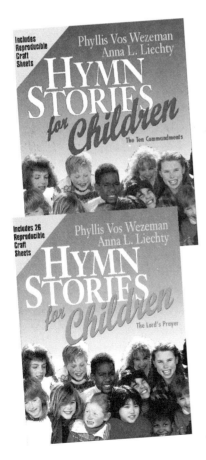

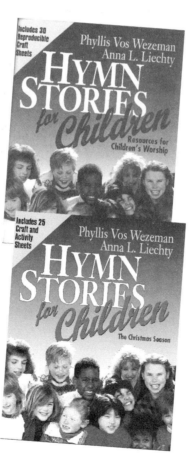

Available now:
- The Apostles' Creed
- Children's Worship
- The Christmas Season
- The Lord's Prayer
- Special Days and Occasions
- The Ten Commandments

Available at your Christian bookstore, or P.O. Box 2607, Grand Rapids, MI 49501